COGNITIVE THERAPY FOR PERSONALITY DISORDERS

Cognitive Therapy for Personality Disorders

A guide for therapists

Kate M Davidson MA, MPhil, PhD
Research Tutor and Consultant Clinical Psychologist,
Department of Psychological Medicine,
Gartnavel Royal Hospital, Glasgow, UK

OXFORD AUCKLAND BOSTON JOHANNESBURG MELBOURNE NEW DELHI

Butterworth-Heinemann
Linacre House, Jordan Hill, Oxford OX2 8DP
225 Wildwood Avenue, Woburn, MA 01801-2041
A division of Reed Educational and Professional Publishing Ltd

℞ A member of the Reed Elsevier plc group

First published 2000

British Library Cataloguing in Publication Data
Davidson, Kate M.
  Cognitive therapy for personality disorders: a guide for
  therapists
  1. Cognitive therapy   2. Personality disorders – Treatment
  I. Title
  616.8′91′42

Library of Congress Cataloguing in Publication Data
A catalogue record of this book is available from the Library of Congress

ISBN 0 7506 4488 5

Typeset by David Gregson Associates, Beccles, Suffolk
Printed and bound in Great Britain

Contents

Foreword by Aaron T Beck   vii

Preface   ix

1   What is personality disorder?   1
2   The cognitive model of personality disorder   15
3   Key characteristics of cognitive therapy for personality disorders   22
4   Basic structure and style of cognitive therapy for personality disorders   33
5   Arriving at a formulation   46
6   Focus on identifying core beliefs   59
7   Focus on changing core beliefs   70
8   Typical behavioural problems: Antisocial personality disorder   81
9   Typical behavioural problems: Borderline personality disorder   94
10   Clinical evaluation of change   107
11   Ending treatment   116
12   Therapy in action: A case illustration of borderline personality disorder   121

Appendix: Core beliefs   145

References   151

Index   157

Foreword

Personality disorders pose a major problem for the clinician. At last we have the volume by Kate Davidson to guide us. In a step-by-step sequence, Dr Davidson takes us through this difficult terrain. She demonstrates how to formulate the case, identify and modify core beliefs and deal with the specific problems of the borderline and antisocial personalities. The illustrative case examples are most illuminating. It is an essential read for both the novice and experienced therapist.

Aaron T Beck, MD
University Professor of Psychiatry
University of Pennsylvania

Preface

This therapist's guide for the treatment of personality disorder is designed to be used by those who have a good understanding of cognitive therapy and can utilize behavioural and cognitive techniques with expertise in the treatment of clients with a variety of mental disorders (Beck *et al.*, 1979; Blackburn and Davidson, 1995). Many individuals with personality disorder enter treatment with disorders such as depression, anxiety or alcohol dependence and therapists quickly become aware that these clients are not responding to treatment as quickly as other clients and that clinical progress seems to be blocked. Therapeutic strategies appear to be only partially effective and the therapist suspects that the client is lacking motivation to change. The interpersonal problems that are so evident in the client's history often manifest themselves in the therapeutic relationship. Although the therapist is aware of these difficulties, the client can appear to have little insight into the effect that these difficulties have on the relationship with the therapist. The client is only aware that these difficulties are consistent with his or her relationships with other people. That is, these difficulties are normal for them.

These characteristics of clients with personality disorder have been observed by Beck and his associates (1990) and by Jeffrey Young (1990) and will be recognizable to clinicians. The long-standing nature of the difficulties and problematic characterological traits that bring these clients to therapy and the resistances which become evident during treatment presents the clinician with a considerable therapeutic challenge requiring high levels of skill and experience.

An earlier version of this treatment guide was used to investigate the efficacy of cognitive therapy in patients with Borderline and Antisocial personality disorder (Davidson and Tyrer, 1996). This study was funded by the Wellcome Trust, and I am grateful to them for allowing me to develop cognitive therapy for this group of clients and to evaluate the impact of carrying out a relatively brief and focused treatment in clients who have traditionally been regarded as difficult to treat. Since that study, I have continued to develop this treatment and I thank those clients who suffered from Borderline and Antisocial personality disorder who have helped me in this endeavour. Their comments and feedback about the acceptability of the therapy and the usefulness of the cognitive and behavioural strategies have been beneficial. Also, my sincere thanks to Aaron Beck, Peter Tyrer, Elizabeth Campbell, Ulrike Schmidt and Paula Keech, who made comments on an earlier draft of the manual, and to Jan Scott who read and commented on the final manuscript.

The procedures outlined in this book are intended to act as guidelines. Experienced clinicians can be flexible and use their own knowledge of cognitive therapy and of the client to select which method of intervention will be the most likely to produce an effective response in alleviating distress and producing appropriate behavioural and cognitive change in their clients with personality disorders.

The book is designed to cover problems and interventions that apply to clients with personality disorder, particularly Antisocial and Borderline personality disorder, but many of the problems and techniques will also apply to clients with other personality disorders. One of the problems in dealing with clients with personality disorder is that one rarely encounters clients who will meet diagnostic criteria for only one personality diagnosis. Rather, a client will have symptoms and problems in common with diagnostic criteria for other personality disorders although one personality disorder may be predominant. Cognitive therapy has been adapted and modified for this group of clients and although further evaluation is required, it appears that clinically important changes can take place with this therapy.

The first chapter provides a brief overview of personality disorder. Chapter 2 introduces the reader to the two best-known cognitive models of personality disorder. Chapters 3 and 4 introduce the reader to the key characteristics of cognitive therapy for personality disorder and how the therapy has been modified and changed to treat individuals with these long-standing problems. Chapters 5–9 provide the clinician with a more detailed account of the specific techniques used in cognitive therapy for personality disorder and how to conceptualize the client's problems within the cognitive model. Assessing clinical change is more difficult with individuals with personality disorder and Chapter 10 is included to provide practitioners with some useful ways of carrying out an evaluation of therapy in a clinical setting. There is a chapter devoted to ending treatment, which is an important issue with clients who may have anxieties about separation and abandonment. Concluding therapy can also be problematic for cognitive therapists who are less familiar with the length of treatment required for individuals with personality disorder and where the client–therapist relationship is more explicit and complex. Chapter 12 is a description of a case.

Although the application of cognitive therapy for those with personality disorders is still in its infancy, it is likely that this approach will be an increasingly important area of clinical and theoretical research in the near future. Clinical work with this group of clients is not for beginners. For the experienced clinician in cognitive therapy, I hope that this book will inspire confidence to help those clients who come to us in distress or cause harm to others by their difficulties.

What is personality disorder?

Interest in abnormal personality has mushroomed since 1980, when the American diagnostic system first described personality disorders (American Psychiatric Association (APA), 1980). These original descriptions were not based on theory but were derived from a consensus agreement amongst informed clinicians and researchers who wished to classify the personality traits seen in clinical settings. In the 1994 *Diagnostic and Statistical Manual*, 4th edition (DSM-IV), the American Psychiatric Association defined personality traits in terms of enduring maladaptive patterns of perceiving, relating to and thinking about the environment and oneself, exhibited in a wide range of important social contexts (APA, 1994). The term personality disorder is used when such personality traits result in impairment in the way an individual functions in a social or occupational context or when these traits result in distress to that individual. These traits are understood to begin in adolescence and be recognizable in adulthood and are therefore regarded as being long-lasting and relatively stable.

There are different views held about the concept of personality disorder (Strack and Lorr, 1997). Implicit in the diagnostic system is the notion that individuals with personality disorder are distinct from those with normal personality by having a physical, biological or genetic abnormality. Not all researchers and clinicians agree with this view and many argue that the distinction between normal and abnormal personality is a matter of degree and that personality traits are more fully and usefully described on dimensions rather than categories. Another view is that compared to those who do not have personality disorder, those with personality disorder share the same personality traits as found in others but these are expressed in a qualitatively different way reflecting a more rigid underlying character structure. Although these conceptualizations differ, they are not mutually exclusive. The cognitive theory of personality disorder gives a central role to schemas and to pre-programmed patterns of behaviour or strategies that through evolution promoted individual survival and reproduction in personality disorder (Beck *et al.*, 1990). It is posited that schemas arise from an interaction between biological predispositional factors and the childhood environment. The underlying cognitive, affective, arousal and motivational patterns or schemas affect the way information about self or the environment is selected and processed.

Assessment of personality disorder

There has been a growth in the number of semi-structured clinical interviews and self-report questionnaires for assessing personality disorder. Table 1.1 describes some of these instruments.

Table 1.1 Measures of personality disorder

Instrument	Type	Authors
International Personality Disorder Examination Revised (PDE-R)	Interview	Loranger *et al.*, 1987, 1994
Structured Clinical Interview for DSM (SCID-II)	Interview (includes a self-report questionnaire as screen)	Spitzer *et al.*, 1990
Structured Interview for DSM-III-R Personality (SIDP-R)	Interview	Tyrer *et al.*, 1988
Personality Diagnostic Questionnaire Revised (PDQ-R) (PDQ-4)	Self-report	Hyler *et al.*, 1988 Hyler, 1994
Millon Clinical Multiaxial Inventory (MCMI-III)	Self-report	Millon *et al.*, 1994
Schedule for Nonadaptive and Adaptive Personality (SNAP)	Self-report	Clark, 1993
Dimensional Assessment of Personality Pathology – Basic Questionnaire (DAPP-BQ)	Self-report	Livesley and Jackson (in press)

Standardized assessments are more reliable than clinician's judgements but there is still no consensus as to how best to assess personality disorder. There appears to be poor agreement between instruments used to assess personality disorder and not all instruments cover all personality disorders. Most interview-based instruments are more reliable when used by trained interviewers with several years' clinical experience. The advantage of interviewing subjects is that the false positive rate for the presence of a personality disorder is likely to be kept to a minimum as the interviewer has the opportunity to ask subsidiary questions to clarify the severity and extent of each personality trait and to make an informed clinical judgement. Also, the degree to which the subject is literate is less problematic in an interview setting whereas literacy level is critical if self-report instruments are used. It is unclear if the same instruments will provide as good reliability if used by independent researchers and it is unclear if patients or informants provide the least biased view of the patient's usual personality traits. In addition, self-report questionnaires appear to give much higher prevalence rates of personality disorder than structured interviews and are probably best used as screening instruments.

Individuals may not recognize the maladaptive nature of their perception, cognition, mood and behaviour and asking an individual to estimate their own degree of abnormality may be problematic if they already have a different baseline of problematic personality traits and behaviour from that which would otherwise be considered normal. Asking an individual to assess their own personality traits requires an ability to self-reflect and an awareness of the degree to which a pattern of thinking, feeling and behaviour is consistent in the self across time. Some traits may be more culturally desirable than others and individuals who are sensitive to perceived social norms and values may alter their endorsement of items according to how they wish to represent themselves and who is enquiring. Partly for this reason, many assessments of personality disorder use reports from knowledgeable informants. Agreement between informants and subjects is however not always high (Bernstein *et al.*, 1997; Zimmerman, 1994).

Although the diagnosis of personality disorder requires that personality traits are enduring, personality traits may fluctuate with the presence of a clinical syndrome and this may distort both the presentation and assessment of traits (Klein, 1993). For example, this problem is particularly apparent in the diagnosis of Borderline personality disorder, in which affective instability is a key feature. Many clients with a diagnosis of Borderline personality disorder suffer from affective disorder or have chronic depressive features which are difficult to separate out from the characteristics of Borderline personality disorder. This has led some researchers to view Borderline personality disorder as an affective spectrum disorder (Akiskal, 1985).

The diagnostic categories of personality disorder have been largely derived from clinical samples where entry into a health care system may have been influenced by the presence of a clinical syndrome or an acute crisis. A more accurate assessment of personality disorder may be obtained by assessing an individual during a period of remission from a clinical disorder or by assessing an individual at more than one point in time. For a thorough review of assessment and related issues the reader is referred to other sources (Jackson, 1998; Weissman, 1993; Zimmerman, 1994).

Dimensional or categorical classifications?

Although current systems of personality disorder classification are categorical, many researchers are critical of this approach. They argue that a dimensional classification may be more appropriate as the boundaries between discrete personality disorders may be artificial and the difference between normal and abnormal personality is better represented as a continuum (Cloninger, 1987; Widiger, 1992). A dimensional view of personality has the advantage of not giving any one trait special significance, of being more comprehensive in its description and in representing personality disturbance in terms of severity rather than categories. In addition, if personality disorders are not dichotomous, then measures which rely on dimensions would include more information than categories and would enable more reliable measurement (Loranger et al., 1994).

Alternative approaches, arising from mainstream academic psychology with its lengthy history of research in personality using psychometric analysis may be clinically useful in describing more fully the negative traits associated with personality disorder. The NEO-PI-R (Costa and McCrae, 1992) has shown that individuals with diagnosable personality disorders differ in predictable ways on the five dimensions of neuroticism, extraversion, openness to experience, agreeableness and conscientiousness (Widiger and Costa, 1994). Other measures of dysfunctional traits, such as the Schedule for Nonadaptive and Adapative Personality (SNAP), which measures traits relevant to personality disorder, may also be useful in investigating theoretical hypotheses on the structure of personality disorder (Clark, 1993). It is clear that there appears to be increasing rapprochement between academic and clinical researchers in this area and it is likely that both normal and abnormal personality will be construed in dimensions but with some overlap between the approaches in the future (Deary and Power, 1998).

Key features of individual personality disorders (DSM-IV)

General criteria

It is important to note that an individual cannot meet criteria for a personality disorder unless the disorder is evident in a broad range of circumstances and has led to significant distress or impairment in social or occupational functioning and is not due to mental or physical illness or due to the physiological effects of drugs. The disorder has to be manifested in at least two of the following domains: thinking, affect, interpersonal relationships and impulse control. In addition, the disorder has to be stable and long-standing and present since early adulthood, if not adolescence.

Paranoid personality disorder

This is characterized by a pervasive distrust and suspiciousness of others who are regarded as malevolent (APA, 1994).

At least four of the following characteristics have to be evident:

- without sufficient basis, is suspicious that others are exploiting, harming or deceiving
- is preoccupied with doubts about trustworthiness or loyalty of others
- is reluctant or fearful of confiding
- reads hidden demeaning or threatening meaning into events
- bears grudges
- perceives others as attacking character
- has recurrent unjustified suspicions regarding fidelity of partner.

Schizoid personality disorder

This is characterized by a pattern of detachment in relationships and a restricted range of emotional expression in interpersonal situations (APA, 1994). At least four of the following characteristics have to be evident:

- avoids close relationships
- chooses solitary activities
- avoids sexual experiences with others

- has few pleasurable activities
- has few close friends or confidantes
- is indifferent to praise or criticism
- is emotionally cold or flat.

Schizotypal personality disorder

This personality disorder is described as 'a pattern of acute discomfort in close relationships' and 'cognitive or perceptual distortions and eccentricities in behaviour' (APA, 1994). At least five of the following characteristics have to be evident:

- ideas of reference
- odd beliefs or magical thinking
- unusual perceptual experiences
- odd thinking or speech
- is suspicious
- inappropriate or restricted affect
- odd, eccentric behaviour or appearance
- no friends or confidantes
- high anxiety in social situations associated with paranoid fears.

Antisocial personality disorder

This disorder is described as 'a pervasive pattern of disregard for and violation of the rights of others' (APA, 1994). Three of the following have to be evident:

- failure to conform to social norms with repeated unlawful behaviour
- deceitfulness
- impulsivity
- aggressiveness and irritability
- disregard for safety of self or others
- irresponsible behaviour
- lack of remorse.

Histrionic personality disorder

This disorder is characterized as a pattern of excessive emotionality and attention-seeking (APA, 1994). At least five of the following criteria have to be evident:

- needs to be centre of attention
- inappropriate sexually seductive behaviour

- shallow expression of emotion
- physical appearance is attention-seeking
- speech style is impressionistic and lacking detail
- exaggerated theatrical expression of emotion
- suggestible
- misjudges closeness in relationships.

Borderline personality disorder

This is a pattern of instability in personal relationships, self-image and affects and marked impulsivity (APA, 1994). At least five of the following criteria have to be evident:

- fear of abandonment
- unstable and intense personal relationships
- identity disturbance
- impulsivity
- recurrent deliberate self-harm
- unstable affect
- feelings of emptiness
- difficulties controlling anger
- stress-related paranoid ideas or dissociation.

Narcissistic personality disorder

This disorder is described as a pattern of grandiosity, need for admiration, with lack of empathy (APA, 1994) At least five of the following characteristics have to be evident:

- grandiose self-importance
- fantasies of success, power, beauty or love
- regards self as special or unique
- need for excessive admiration
- sense of entitlement
- exploitative interpersonally
- lacks empathy
- envious
- arrogant.

Avoidant personality disorder

This is described as a 'pattern of social inhibition, feelings of inadequacy, and hypersensitivity to negative evaluation' (APA, 1994). At least four of the following characteristics have to be evident:

- avoids activities involving interpersonal contact
- only becomes involved if certainty that will be liked by others
- restrained in interpersonal relationships
- fears criticism or ridicule
- feelings of inadequacy in new interpersonal situations
- views self as socially inept or inferior
- reluctant to take personal risks because of fear of embarrassment.

Dependent personality disorder

This is characterized as a 'pattern of excessive need to be taken care of that leads to submissive behaviour and fears of separation' (APA, 1994). At least five of the following characteristics have to be evident:

- requires excessive reassurance to make everyday decisions
- need for others to assume responsibility
- fears disagreeing with others
- lacks confidence initiating activities
- excessive need for nurturance
- fear of being alone
- quickly seeks another close relationship if one ends
- fear of abandonment.

Obsessive–compulsive personality disorder

This is a 'pattern of preoccupation with orderliness, perfectionism, and mental and interpersonal control at the expense of flexibility, openness and efficiency' (APA, 1994). At least four of the following characteristics have to be evident:

- preoccupation with rules and detail
- perfectionism
- overemphasis on work and productivity at the expense of relationships and leisure activities
- overconscientious
- hoards objects
- unable to delegate
- miserliness
- rigidity and stubbornness.

Personality disorder not otherwise specified

This category in DSM-IV (APA, 1994) is for disorders of personality where an individual may have several of the characteristics of different personality disorders but does not fit any one of the specific personality disorders listed above.

Classification systems

In the American diagnostic system, personality disorders and clinical syndromes such as major depression, anxiety disorders and schizophrenia are diagnosed on different dimensions or axes. Personality disorders are diagnosed on Axis II in DSM-IV (APA, 1994) whereas clinical syndromes are diagnosed on Axis I. The implication of making personality disorder diagnoses on a separate axis is that this type of disorder is thought to exist continuously from late adolescence and is not associated with a condition that is characterized by a relapsing course or that remits like a typical illness syndrome. Rather an individual with a diagnosis of personality disorder will display attributes that are relatively enduring and persistent and is unlikely to show much variation in that the traits will be observed in a wide number of environmental and interpersonal contexts. This results in a lack of flexibility and adaptability as the individual has a narrow and limited range of coping styles.

In the International Classification of Diseases system (ICD-10; WHO, 1992), personality disorders are coded on the same axis as mental disorders. This classification system is similar to DSM except that different names are used for broadly similar types of personality disorders and in each system there are a number of disorders that do not appear in the other. For example, ICD-10 uses the term Dissocial to describe the personality disorder referred to as Antisocial in DSM-IV, Anankastic personality disorder in ICD-10 is referred to as Obsessive–compulsive in DSM-IV and Anxious personality disorder is referred to as Avoidant in DSM-IV. Narcissistic and Passive aggressive personality disorders are not found in ICD-10.

In addition, unlike ICD-10, DSM-IV has grouped personality disorders into clusters, with the assumption that these clusters may have some shared attributes. DSM-IV personality disorder clusters are as shown in Table 1.2.

How common is personality disorder?

Community estimates of personality disorder may misclassify individuals or overestimate the prevalence of personality disorder in the community. This is partly because information from other sources is not accessed, and individuals are assessed usually by completing questionnaires asking about the presence or absence of a particular

Table 1.2   DSM-IV personality disorder clusters

DSM cluster	Personality disorder
Cluster A Odd or eccentric	Paranoid
	Schizoid
	Schizotypal
Cluster B Flamboyant and dramatic	Antisocial
	Borderline
	Narcissistic
	Histrionic
Cluster C Fearful or anxious	Avoidant
	Dependent
	Obsessive–compulsive

trait or behaviour. In the United States, estimates of the prevalence rates of any DSM-III personality disorder range from 10.3 to 11.1 per 100 in surveys of non- clinical populations (Zimmerman and Coryell, 1990; Reich et al., 1989) using the self- report Personality Diagnostic Questionnaire (PDQ) (Hyler et al., 1983). Using a two- stage method in which only subjects who were screened as positive for personality disorder on a self-completion personality disorder inventory were interviewed by clinicians, the point-prevalence estimate for DSM-III-R personality disorder in a student population obtained a similar rate of 11.01% (Lenzenweger et al., 1997).

Cluster A prevalence

When prevalence rates of categories of personality disorders are investigated in community samples, the rates vary with the specific personality disorder, the sample size, the method of sampling and the assessment measure utilized. Within Cluster A, Schizotypal is the most prevalent personality disorder in this group (up to 5.6 per 100) and Paranoid personality disorder appears to be least prevalent, with reported rates of between 0.4 and 1.8 per 100 (Weissman, 1990).

Cluster B prevalence

In Cluster B (Antisocial, Histrionic, Borderline and Narcissistic), Antisocial personality disorder has the highest prevalence rate, varying from 2.1 to 3.7 per 100 in a North American community sample (Widiger and Corbitt, 1995). This diagnosis is associated with notably higher rates in males compared to females and higher rates in younger as opposed to older males. In community surveys Narcissistic personality disorder is low in prevalence, with two studies reporting a rate of 0.4 per 100 (Reich *et al.*, 1989; Zimmerman and Coryell, 1990). One study carried out as part of the Epidemiological Catchment Area program (ECA) in Baltimore, USA, found a prevalence rate of 2.2% for Histrionic personality disorder using DSM-III criteria and noted no sex difference for this diagnosis in those under the age of 45 years. However, for those over this age, the prevalence rate in women compared to men was over eight times higher (Nestadt *et al.*, 1990). In addition, 17% of the women with Histrionic personality disorder also suffered from depression and they noted a higher rate of suicide attempts and use of medical services compared to those without this personality disorder. The prevalence rate of Borderline personality disorder varies between 0.2 and 4.6 per 100 depending on the survey and whether point or lifetime prevalence is assessed (Weissman, 1990). In general, the diagnosis of Borderline personality disorder is associated with being young, single and female, and with relatively high rates of alcohol and tobacco use, suicide attempts, and comorbid diagnosis of schizophrenia and phobias as well as other personality disorders (Zimmerman and Coryell, 1990). Individuals in this group have been found to be high users of mental health services, and are associated with poor marital relationships, work difficulties, alcohol-related problems and psychosexual problems (Swartz *et al.*, 1990).

Cluster C prevalence

Within Cluster C (Avoidant, Dependent, Compulsive, Passive aggressive), Reich *et al.* (1989) found no cases of Avoidant personality disorder among relatives of control probands and Zimmerman and Coryell (1990) reported low rates of between 0.4 and 1.3 per 100 depending on which instrument was used at assessment. Dependent personality disorder is more prevalent, with rates of between 1.6 and 6.7% being reported, with lower rates being reported when structured interviews are utilized (Weissman, 1990). Using the PDQ, Zimmerman and Coryell (1990) reported a prevalence rate of 4 per 100 for Obsessive–compulsive personality disorder and again a lower rate of 1.7 per 100 with a structured interview. Untypical of personality disorders, this disorder is more common among educated, married individuals (Nestadt *et al.*, 1991). Using the PDQ, Zimmermann and Coryell (1990) found a low rate of Passive aggressive personality disorder (0.4 per 100), but when direct interview was used this rate rose to 3 per 100, which suggests that individuals with this type of disorder may under-report on self-report measures.

Prevalence of personality disorders in psychiatric populations

When prevalence rates of personality disorder are investigated in psychiatric populations, it is clear that patients not only have more personality disturbance and disorder but also suffer from clinical syndromes and disorders in addition to personality disorder. Studies have found variable rates depending on the sampling procedure used, the diagnostic criteria utilized, the assessment instruments employed and other factors such as admission policies and availability of services. Borderline, Schizotypal and Histrionic personality disorders are commonly found in samples of treated patients, many of whom may require admission to hospital, or intensive psychiatric care due to the level of severity of psychological and social impairment. In outpatient samples, Dependent and Passive aggressive personality disorders are also commonly found (Girolamo and Reich, 1993). With the introduction of diagnostic tools for personality disorder with DSM-III, these disorders are increasingly recognized and diagnosed. For example, in one large teaching hospital in the United States, the percentage of patients with a diagnosis of personality disorder rose from 19% to 49% over two 5-year periods before and after the introduction of DSM-III (Loranger, 1990).

Comorbidity

Feinstein (1970) introduced the term 'comorbidity', defined as 'any distinct additional clinical entity that has existed or that may occur during the clinical course of a patient who has the index disease under study' (p. 456). The term comorbid is restricted to diseases or disorders and, strictly speaking, does not apply to symptoms. There are several uses of the term comorbidity in psychiatric research and practice (Maser and Cloninger, 1990). Clinical studies use the concept of comorbidity to describe the fact that more than one disorder can be diagnosed in the same individual, whereas in psychiatric epidemiological studies, the term is used to indicate the relative risk of disorders, other than the index disorder, being present within an individual patient. One of the difficulties of working either clinically or as a researcher in the area of personality disorders is that comorbidity is extremely common, both with other personality disorders and with clinical syndromes and disorders (Tyrer, 1999). This has several implications. For the clinician, it means that they are likely to encounter considerable overlap between different personality disorders, with patients meeting criteria for several personality disorders or patients who have several seriously dysfunctional personality traits but who do not meet criteria for any one specific personality disorder. Some have suggested that the diagnostic categories themselves have low specificity but it might also suggest that personality disorder and dysfunction is an integral part of pathology experienced by patients attending psychiatric services.

Can psychological treatment help?

There are an increasing number of treatment approaches to personality disorder but few have been systematically evaluated to date, except Dialectical Behaviour Therapy (DBT) (Linehan *et al.*, 1991; Linehan *et al.*, 1993). This intensive treatment for Borderline personality disorder includes behavioural, cognitive and psychodynamic elements as well as techniques based on meditation. Compared to treatment as usual, those women who received DBT did significantly better during treatment and during the 6 months after treatment had ended but no differences were found between the two groups in the number of parasuicidal episodes after 6 months post-treatment (Linehan et al., 1993). Psychodynamic therapies have been modified to accommodate patients with personality disorder as traditional approaches were not helpful (Dowson and Grounds, 1995) and more modern approaches allow the therapist to be more active and directive but again there are no controlled trials of this approach to testify to its efficacy. Apart from these studies, evaluation of treatment effectiveness comes from single case studies. For example, case studies provide some evidence that behaviour therapy, cognitive therapy and cognitive analytical therapy can be helpful in improving relationships and in reducing dysfunctional behaviour (e.g. Ryle, 1997; Turkat and Maisto, 1985) including self-harm (Davidson and Tyrer, 1996).

How do we explain personality disorder to our patients?

It is doubtful if the label personality disorder is helpful to an individual with such a disorder. It may even be counterproductive in a treatment setting, as well as potentially alarming to that individual and to others. If research in this area was more developed and we knew more about the longer-term consequences and treatability of these disorders, then using the label personality disorder might be a different matter. At present, we have to consider what the label might mean to an individual. To many, it might imply that there is nothing they can do to change as personality is generally thought of as being fundamental to one's concept of self and therefore stable and unchangeable. The label has a pejorative connotation and this may imply a defective condition. There are undoubtedly personality disorders which are more dysfunctional than others; the distinction between a disorder such as Avoidant personality disorder and Antisocial personality disorder may be meaningful to the clinician but to the layman, the salient term may be 'personality disorder' and the distinctions between disorders, less salient and meaningful.

That some individuals with personality disorder come to us distressed about their condition is incontrovertible. Some come because others have urged them to seek help and they may not appear to be distressed by the effect they have on others. However, even they may be aware that changing their behaviour and thinking could have positive consequences. Our assessment of their problems, both current and historical, gives us the opportunity to explain to them why we believe they suffer from a personality disorder but we have to be able to explain this in a way that makes sense to the patient, is non-pejorative, and allows the possibility that change is possible.

How can cognitive therapy help?

Working within a cognitive model is helpful in that it allows a conceptualization of the disorder that can be shared with and understood by the patient. Habitual maladaptive behaviours and dysfunctional beliefs have a negative impact on interpersonal relationships and places a limit on the quality of life it is possible to experience. Most individuals recognize these maladaptive patterns and most come to believe that if they could make changes in these areas, the quality of their lives could be improved. The onus is on us to explain that this is what is meant by the term personality disorder and why we believe someone who has such maladaptive behaviours and relationships can change.

Through the formulation of the client's problems, cognitive therapy allows us to help our clients develop a better understanding of how earlier life experience may have influenced their extreme views of themselves and others. The interpersonal problems and behavioural difficulties which are so common can be likewise understood and modified as new ways of perceiving, thinking and behaving can be tested out within the relatively safe environment of therapy. Cognitive therapy allows us to both explain personality disorder and work with the client collaboratively to make changes in behaviour and thinking.

2

The cognitive model of personality disorder

When formulating a case and carrying out therapy, it is essential that we have a model to guide our understanding of the client's difficulties. Aaron Beck and his associates and Jeffrey Young have developed cognitive models of personality disorder which are both informative and useful for therapists and theorists. Although both these models emphasize childhood environmental influences as being important in the development of dysfunctional schemas, Beck's model brings an evolutionary perspective to bear on the origins of personality disorder.

Beck and his associates

Individuals with personality disorder are characterized by an inner experience and ingrained behaviour that deviates from that which is expected in the individual's culture. Beck and his associates (1990), taking an evolutionary perspective, suggest that humans and animals demonstrate some behaviours which are genetically determined or 'programmed'. The overt behaviour which is observable is the product of these programmes and is shaped by the interaction between genetics and the environment. These programmes involve cognitive processing, affect, action, self-regulation and motivation and are likely to have evolved as a result of being essential to survival and reproduction.

It is thought that these programmes influence automatic processes such as perception, affective and action responses. In personality disorder, behaviours that were adaptive and had survival value in more primitive settings have become problematic in the present culture because they may conflict with the prevailing norms of that society. For example, competitive behaviour might be appropriate in an environment where there are limited resources and rewards but will be excessive and inappropriate in a society which has sufficient resources and where there is a high value placed on social cohesion. This poor fit between programmed strategies and environment may be a factor in the development of maladaptive patterns of behaviour and traits in individuals who are diagnosed as 'personality disorder'. It is not that these strategies are necessarily inappropriate in themselves, it is more that they become maladaptive when they are exhibited in a rigid and inflexible manner and are not inhibited in situations when this would be adaptive. It may be useful, for example, to be dramatic in some situations, such as teaching, where one has to get the attention of others, but such behaviour may not be fitting in other situations that require sensitivity and reciprocity. In those with personality disorder, certain behavioural strategies appear to be overdeveloped and used inflexibly and rigidly and are therefore not adaptive to situations as they are not used selectively.

Beck's model of personality disorder places importance on the interaction of the individual's environment with biological predispositions and the temperamental tendencies of the individual which are present at birth. Through experience, certain types of behaviours and attitudes will become exaggerated or minimized. The child whose temperament is naturally shy may develop clinging behaviour, which may in turn generate a response from others which is overly protective and nurturing. As the child develops, she may come to believe that she cannot survive without the protection of others and help-seeking and dependent behaviour become increasingly accentuated and others are perceived as dangerous and malevolent.

Just as clinical syndromes or disorders can be conceived of in terms of evolutionary principles of survival and adaptation, such as the fight/flight pattern of response in anxiety disorders, Beck *et al.*, (1990) consider that personality disorders could be regarded as an exaggeration of patterns of behaviour that promote individual survival and reproduction. They also suggest that the natural variability in the gene pool could account for individual differences in personality which may have specific survival value. For example, one individual may appear sexually provocative whereas another makes no attempt at appearing attractive or seductive in a situation in which gaining the protection of a dominant male may be an advantage. The behaviours themselves may elicit a variety of different responses in others and these differences may have different survival value in certain situations.

In the cognitive model of personality disorder, these patterns of behaviour or strategies are related to underlying cognitive, affective, motivational, action and self-regulatory schemas (see Figure 2.1). Cognitive therapy is based on information processing theory which asserts that schemas develop as a means of organizing experience and are part of normal cognitive development. The products of schemas will reflect concepts of self and others. Cognitive theory suggests that in personality disorder, maladaptive schemas are hypervalent and thus evoked across many situations and are thought to drive overt behavioural strategies which may be dysfunctional in specific environments.

For example, it is likely that an individual with an Antisocial personality disorder who exhibits aggressive and combative behaviour will hold a core belief that other people are there to be exploited. The tendency to 'act now and think later' will be linked to an overdeveloped action schema and an underdeveloped self-regulatory and monitoring schema. For other personality disorders, such as Borderline personality disorder, the association between core beliefs and behavioural strategies will be similar but the content different as illustrated in Table 2.1. Often individuals with Borderline personality disorder will oscillate between two opposing behavioural strategies, such as dependency and avoidance of intimacy with others, in association with incompatible beliefs, such as 'I cannot cope on my own' and 'No one will ever love me'.

Table 2.1 Core beliefs and associated behavioural strategies in Antisocial and Borderline personality disorder

Typical core beliefs	*Behavioural strategies*	
	Over-developed	*Under-developed*
Borderline personality disorder		
I am bad	Self-punishment	Self-nurturance
No one will ever love me	Avoidance of closeness	Openness to relationships
I cannot cope on my own	Over-dependence	Independence
Antisocial personality disorder		
I can do what I want	Autonomous	Sharing
Other people will get in my way	Combative	Group identification
Don't get close to others	Self-sufficiency	Intimacy

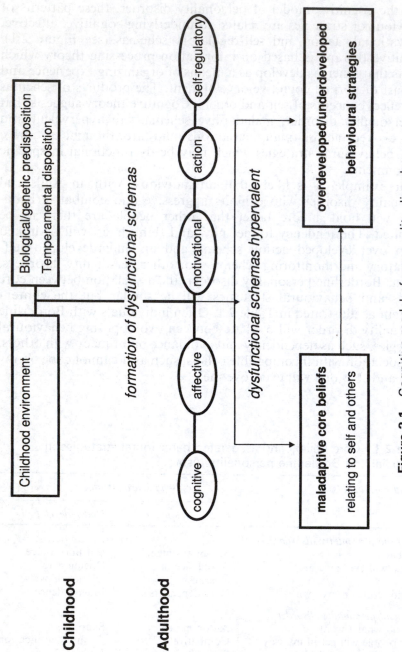

Figure 2.1 Cognitive model of personality disorder

Young's early maladaptive schemas

Schemas develop in response to biological predispositions and environmental influences. For example, particular schemas develop in response to early relationships with family members. Young (1990) has introduced the concept of early maladaptive schemas (EMS). The content of these schemas is concerned with self-identity and relationships with others and is developed during childhood and elaborated throughout one's life. EMS are the cumulative result of early dysfunctional experiences with people in the child's immediate environment (Young and Lindemann, 1992). Each schema is thought to comprise of cognitive, affective and inter-personal components. These schemas are concerned with themes relating to hypothesized developmental stages of personality. The most common themes noted relate to the need for security, autonomy, desirability, self-expression, gratification and self-control. Cognitive therapy for personality disorder aims to modify these early maladaptive schemas.

Schemas in therapy

These are also referred to as unconditional core schemas or beliefs and are regarded as being capable of generating high levels of distress as the schemas are a core part of cognitive organization and encode experience and memory associated with affective states. As these schemas are central to one's sense of self-identity and are egosyntonic, any attempt at changing these schemas may result in an increase in levels of distress. Schemas that relate to self-identity are likely to be resistant to change and may impede therapy that aims at challenging these.

The goal of therapy is to identify schemas which are maladaptive and which prevent the individual from functioning in an adaptive manner. The schemas which are focused on during therapy concern core concepts about the self and others. The content and meaning of the schemas affect interpersonal relationships, including the therapeutic relationship. Young has developed an instrument for assessing EMS called the Schema Questionnaire (Young, 1990). This can be productive in generating an initial list of potential dysfunctional beliefs and in monitoring change in clients.

Young (1990) has proposed that schemas are reinforced through the three different processes: schema maintenance, schema avoidance and schema compensation.

Schema maintenance

This is the process by which information or evidence that would disconfirm the schema are resisted through cognitive distortions and by self-defeating behavioural patterns. This type of information processing appears to be common in clients with personality disorders. It is as if the client cannot accommodate new information that would not fit with what they believe to be true of themselves or others. Information that would appear to be evidence that would directly disconfirm a belief is readily dismissed or discounted and may even appear to be totally ignored. One example of this type of processing comes from a client with a Borderline personality disorder who believed that she was worthless. She could not make sense of several women at work repeatedly inviting her to go out with them, even though she kept refusing. Her explanation for the invitations was that her colleagues somehow knew that she had no friends and felt sorry for her or that they might need another person to make up numbers. Alternative explanations such as that they might want to get to know her better were given no consideration and dismissed as being impossible as she thought that everyone, including her colleagues, could see by looking at her that she was boring, worthless and had nothing to say. She could not conceive that her colleagues might have been acting in a genuinely friendly manner towards her.

Schema avoidance

When maladaptive schemas are activated, intense negative emotions are experienced which are so unpleasant that individuals will automatically attempt to suppress or avoid triggering the schema or the unpleasant affect associated with the schema. Avoidance can operate at a cognitive level where clients will either not want to speak or think about an event which would bring a schema into sharp focus. Other avoidance tactics include suppressing or dulling down feelings (affective avoidance) and overt behavioural avoidance. A client, with a diagnosis of Antisocial personality disorder, who held the dysfunctional belief that he was superior to others, avoided any challenges to this belief by never putting himself in the position of finding work which would have provided evidence of his talents and abilities. These processes of avoidance prevent opportunities for schemas to be modified and thus the subjective belief in negative schemas is reinforced.

Schema compensation

An individual may overcompensate for a negative schema by acting in the direction opposite to the schema's content. This process can sometimes be functional. For example, a female client with a schema concerning defectiveness and unattractiveness might behave in a manner that demands attention and admiration from men. However, her attempts are likely to backfire as she is unlikely to be able to modify her behaviour appropriately and may get involved with men who may ultimately reject her, thus confirming her belief that she is unattractive.

3

Key characteristics of cognitive therapy for personality disorders

In cognitive therapy for personality disorders, there are some important differences in characteristics and emphasis when a comparison is made with cognitive therapy for the emotional disorders. Before emphasizing the main differences, it may be useful to briefly summarize the main components of cognitive therapy for the emotional disorders. There are many components which are shared and are evident in cognitive therapy for personality disorder. A comparison of cognitive therapy for clinical disorders and personality disorders is outlined in Table 3.1.

Cognitive therapy for emotional disorders

Cognitive therapy has many distinct advantages over some other forms of psychotherapy. It is a brief, time-limited treatment and the techniques used are readily accessible to clients and easily learnt by therapists. Taking depression as an example, cognitive behaviour therapy has been extensively evaluated and has been found to be at least as effective as pharmacological treatments and other forms of psychotherapy in ameliorating the symptoms in depression (for example, Hollon *et al.*; 1992, Murphy *et al.*, 1984), and most importantly, it can reduce the likelihood of relapse (Blackburn *et al.*, 1986; Evans *et al.*, 1992; Shea *et al.*, 1992; Simons *et al.*, 1986).

In depression, individuals experience a bewildering array of changes to normal functioning. Someone with depression may experience extreme feelings of sadness and hopelessness, have difficulties concentrating, experience low self-esteem, suicidal thoughts,

Table 3.1 Differences in style and characteristics of therapy

	Clinical disorders	*Personality disorders*
Length of treatment	3–4 months	9 months or more
Pace of treatment	Brisk	Variable
Problem time scale	Here and now	Here and now and lifetime
Therapeutic relationship	Collaborative	Collaborative; clear client–therapist boundaries
Problem content	Client's world, present and future	Client's world, past, present and future therapeutic relationship
Problem focus	Behaviour Cognition Emotion	Behaviour Cognition Emotion The therapeutic relationship
Emphasis in intervention	Automatic thoughts	Behaviour Schemas
Homework	Automatic thoughts data collection	Behavioural data collection Reworking of beliefs
Scientific method	Experimental	Experimental
Learning model	Maladaptive learning	Maladaptive learning or failure to learn through lack of appropriate opportunity
Openness	Explicit	Explicit, rule bound

guilt and shame and ruminate over past negative experiences and memories. They may have difficulty motivating themselves to do things and have problems carrying out tasks due to being slowed down or agitated. Behavioural avoidance is common. In addition, they will experience changes in bodily functions such as sleep problems, appetite and sexual desire and performance. Depressed individuals selectively attend to the most negative aspects of themselves, perceive their world as making overwhelming demands and view their futures as bleak and unchanging.

Table 3.2 Systematic logical errors

Logical error	Definition
Selective abstraction	Focusing on one aspect of a situation whilst other more relevant information is ignored
Arbitrary inference	Drawing a conclusion in the absence of sufficient evidence
Over-generalization	Drawing a general conclusion on the basis of one aspect of a situation or an isolated case
Magnification and minimization	Exaggerating the importance of events or discounting positive aspects of an event
Personalization	Relating external events to oneself when there is no basis for making such a connection

Negative automatic thoughts

Beck's cognitive theory of the emotional disorders emphasizes three related components: negative automatic thoughts, logical errors or distortions and dysfunctional schemas. Negative automatic thoughts are those fleeting negative thoughts which occur just outside the focus of immediate awareness but which are accessible to the individual once drawn to their attention. The content of these thoughts is negative in tone and may include images, daydreams, memories and specific verbal thoughts. The individual does not question whether the content of these automatic thoughts are true.

Systematic thinking errors

These are the distortions or errors in cognitive processing which maintain the negative bias in the content of thought in depression. These errors systematically bias the way information from the environment is interpreted. The most common thinking errors which describe the cognitive processes of depressed clients are outlined in Table 3.2. These categories are not necessarily mutually exclusive. In addition, the difference between normal and pathological processing is a matter of the frequency with which these errors occur and the extent and degree of bias.

Dysfunctional schemas

Schemas are stable knowledge structures which represent an individual's total knowledge of self and the world. This knowledge will be based on the individual's past as well as more recent experience and any new information is processed through schemas. In depression, depressogenic schemas may have been developed over many years but will only be evident when activated by stressful events or low mood. For example, a depressed woman may hold a depressogenic assumption or belief concerned with motherhood such as 'If I am a good mother, my children will be happy and successful'. If her child then becomes unhappy and does poorly at school, such events would be likely to be perceived as stressful and the dysfunctional schema concerned with motherhood which was previously dormant would become activated. As the schema becomes activated, it is applied to a variety of situations and contexts and there would be an increase in the negative bias in information processing. This, in turn, will lead to an increasingly negative affective state, which would further increase the negative cognitive bias in perception. Without any ameliorating factors to counter this process, this individual would become depressed.

Cognitive behaviour therapy for the emotional disorders is designed to deal with these negative automatic thoughts, assumptions and beliefs (Beck *et al.*, 1979). Individuals are taught how to monitor and evaluate their negative thinking. Through guided discovery, therapists aim to decrease the bias in thinking and to coach the client to challenge their negative thoughts by becoming aware of alternative, more reality-based, views of the same situation. Therapists encourage their clients to test out the reality of their negative thoughts or assumptions through behavioural tasks. Clients are encouraged to practise coping skills in situations in which they would have previously had difficulties and they learn to become more adept at problem-solving. Therapists aim to provide some understanding of underlying dysfunctional beliefs and the impact of these on the individual. As clients with emotional disorders such as depression have access to more functional non-depressogenic beliefs and have not always experienced depression-related problems, they can more readily access alternative more adaptive schemas and have within their behavioural repertoire, adaptive coping behaviours and skills. For those with personality disorder, there is no alternative experience of self and the world and no flexibility in behavioural strategies. The dysfunctional core beliefs which are so evident in those with personality disorder are long-standing and there is no alternative more adaptive belief which is accessible. For the therapist, the task is to engage the client with personality disorder in finding less absolute and more adaptive beliefs and behaviours. The therapy therefore needs to be adjusted to aid this process.

Key differences in cognitive therapy for personality disorders

There are five main differences in emphasis in cognitive therapy for personality disorders: these concern the central importance and function of formulation in guiding therapy, the nature of the client–therapist relationship, the emphasis on core beliefs and the importance placed on behavioural change to promote changes in beliefs about self and others. In addition, not all cognitive therapists may want to, or have the skills necessary to, treat individuals with personality disorder. Included here is a speculative list of the qualities and attributes which may be desirable in therapists.

Formulation

The most important therapeutic tool is the therapist's formulation of the client's problems within a cognitive framework. A formulation, in the case of personality disorder, is essentially a hypothesis which ties together the client's long-standing problematic behaviours, interpersonal problems and hypothesized underlying dysfunctional core beliefs which have arisen largely as a result of childhood experiences. The first stage of therapy involves arriving at a formulation. This is explicitly shared with the client and helps both the therapist and client to understand the client's difficulties. It has a pragmatic application in determining which strategies are likely to be the most useful in promoting effective change in the client. Arriving at a formulation also helps the therapist to anticipate where difficulties might arise in therapy and inform the therapist of potential difficulties in establishing a relationship with the client and what mechanisms underlie the client's problems and where behavioural and attitudinal changes can most readily be made. It takes time to develop a formulation as it includes a historical account of the difficulties experienced. Although it is possible to arrive at an adequate working formulation in three sessions, it can take more sessions to fully understand the links between past and present problems. Not infrequently, a therapist may change an initial formulation later in therapy as further information and details become available.

One important aspect of the formulation in cognitive therapy for personality disorders is that it is shared with the client and made explicit. This allows both the therapist and client to work from the same canvas. Both client and therapist can collaborate on what needs to change and the client benefits from having a model which makes sense of how their problems may have arisen and been maintained. Without an adequate formulation, the therapist will tend to carry out treatment on a problem by problem basis and as clients with personality disorders have a tendency to present the therapist with a shifting array of problems, the therapy may never proceed to any satisfactory conclusion. More detail on developing a formulation is to be found in Chapter 5.

The client–therapist relationship

As individuals with personality disorders tend to have a wide array of problems, including difficulties in establishing constructive relationships, therapists can begin to feel overwhelmed and negative about their relationships with these clients. Treating individuals with personality disorder does require considerable clinical skill and experience, an ability to work in a structured way and the ability to formulate the client's problems within a theoretical model of therapy to guide treatment. To expect all clinicians who come into contact with clients with personality disorder to have the above characteristics is clearly unrealistic. It is not uncommon, for example, to find well-meaning therapists who overcompensate by putting more and more diffuse efforts into trying to be helpful to the client with the result that the main goals in therapy become lost and the boundaries of the therapeutic relationship become blurred. This almost inevitably leads to more problems as there is a drift away from clear goals, increasing confusion of expectations within the therapeutic relationship and less overall resolution of problems. As a result, many therapists feel at a loss when faced with such clients and are unlikely to effect any change in their clients who may then suffer more as a result of having seemingly failed in treatment and in addition, may find themselves alienated from service providers. There is a need for therapists to acquire the necessary skills and knowledge to engage and treat this group of clients so that the clients themselves can benefit and are not merely labelled as difficult or even untreatable.

The general stance of the cognitive therapist working with clients with personality disorders is one of openness and interest in the client. The therapist should be clear about the aim of therapy, which is to increase adaptive behaviour and thinking and to decrease maladaptive behaviours and modify dysfunctional rigid core beliefs. This clarity is essential to the therapist in that it prevents the therapist from being drawn into condoning potential negative and self-defeating behaviours and beliefs in the client. The therapist aids the client to do the right thing at the right time and to act in such as way as to promote adaptive self-enhancing behaviours.

One of the hallmarks of an individual with a personality disorder is the presence of persistent interpersonal difficulties. Just as individuals

with personality disorders have difficulties understanding and nego-
tiating interpersonal relationships, these same difficulties are likely to
manifest themselves within the client–therapist relationship. The
therapist needs to be aware of these problems in carrying out
treatment and has to be sensitive to the relationship difficulties that
can arise between them and the client. This highlights an important
difference between treatment of clinical disorders (Axis I) such as
anxiety and depression and the treatment of personality disorders:
the therapeutic relationship itself can become a focus of treatment in
personality disorder if there are problems with engagement in therapy
or serious disruptions to progress in therapy which arise from
misinterpretations of either the client or therapist's expectations,
motives or behaviour.

Persons and Bertagnolli (1994) have suggested that keeping
therapy focused on overt problems aids the development of a
collaborative relationship. In cognitive therapy for individuals with
personality disorder, the emphasis is on change to both underlying
core beliefs and self-defeating behaviours or behaviours which may
cause harm to others. By sharing the cognitive formulation with a
client, the relationship between core beliefs and long-standing
maladaptive behaviours is relatively easily comprehended by clients
and concentrating on the overt difficulties relating to core beliefs aids
both the change process and a collaborative style in therapy. One of
the main emphases therefore is on identifying and modifying self-
defeating behaviours or behaviours that disrupt relationships.
Encouraging the client to endorse and experience the advantages of
modifying these behaviours promotes a positive working alliance
with the therapist.

Very few clients with personality disorders come to therapy with
the expressed aim of changing their personality traits. Rather they are
referred with problems such as failing to maintain relationships,
getting into trouble with the police, repeatedly self-harming and
experiencing high levels of distress that cannot readily be accounted
for by their circumstances. Once the main problems have been
established and phrased in a way that positive and adaptive change
can be recognized and assessed, the aims of treatment are readily
apparent and there is less room for misunderstanding to develop.
Difficulties that appear to be related to the therapist–client relationship can likewise be treated as problems to be resolved.

The relationship laboratory

In cognitive therapy, therapists can use the relationship between
themselves and their clients as a 'relationship laboratory'. Therapists

have an opportunity to observe a client's interpersonal behaviour at first hand as well as gaining a historical account of persistent difficulties in other relationships. Although cognitive therapy does not use the therapeutic relationship as a vehicle for change in itself, as in some forms of psychodynamic therapy, the client–therapist relationship can be utilized either directly, or as an example of relationships with others, if there are problems with engagement or progress in treatment due to potential misinterpretations about the relationship.

The following example of how the client–therapist relationship is utilized in a situation which would disrupt therapy may be helpful. A client with an Antisocial personality disorder presented behaviours which interfered with progress in therapy and were unacceptable in a clinical setting. On two consecutive occasions, he arrived late for his appointments and on the second occasion he became angry and verbally hostile to clinic reception staff who drew his attention to the fact he was late again. Other clients in the waiting area complained to staff and were clearly rather frightened by his explosive behaviour. In addition, the therapist observed that he attempted to change the topic when talking about difficulties in his relationship with his partner who had left him for another man whilst he was in prison. The former of these incidents threatened the viability of him attending the clinic and the latter hampered progress in therapy. His behaviour towards the therapist and reception staff and his lack of punctuality had to be addressed if therapy was to continue. The therapist explicitly told him why this issue was being addressed and that she had to understand what his difficulties were in attending on time and in discussing his relationship with his partner as he had stated he wanted help in maintaining relationships. The therapist asked him to view his behaviour from the perspective of herself and others. She asked him to think about the disadvantages of being late for appointments and how he thought she might view his late attendance and how others might react to his shouting verbal abuse in the waiting area. At first, he found the task of taking the perspective of another difficult but eventually, he became aware that his behaviour in the waiting area might be regarded as inappropriate as he saw no one else behaving in this manner. With regard to being late for appointments and not keeping on topic in sessions, it became apparent that he held a belief that he should always be the 'one with the upper hand' in relationships and he had to show people who was in charge by his dominant or aggressive behaviour otherwise he would be 'pushed around by others'.

The above theme was evident in his history. He had little experience of collaborative relationships and his behavioural strategies and attitudes towards others would have mitigated against cooperation. His childhood had been both emotionally and economically deprived. He had not known his father, and his mother had lived with several men, some of whom had beaten and humiliated him. Other than being beaten, for the most part he had been neglected. His only way to establish some sense of identity had been through his peer group. It was with them that he learnt to fight and behave aggressively in order to get what he wanted which was mostly some validation that he existed and could have some influence over others. Clearly an early task in therapy was to reach some joint understanding of this problem through evaluating his basic belief about being 'in charge' and as one of his goals in therapy was to improve his relationships with others, he agreed to keep an open mind about the effectiveness of aggressive behaviour as a means of getting what he wanted. He attempted to change his behaviour towards the therapist and agreed to stick to the agenda as an experiment. If he wanted to learn how to approach people in a manner to gain their respect and cooperation, then it was pointed out to him that his relationship with the therapist would be a good starting point. He would get honest feedback and help to improve his social skills and any fears which he had about not being 'in charge' could be evaluated. Had the therapist not brought these difficulties into the main agenda for therapy, the therapy would most likely have reached an early impasse.

Therapist qualities and skills

There may be some attributes and skills which make some therapists more suitable than others in dealing with clients with personality problems. The following are some personal attributes and skills which may be helpful.

- A thorough understanding of the theoretical framework of cognitive therapy.
- Experience in treating a wide range of clients using cognitive behavioural therapy.
- A personal therapeutic style which is collaborative, warm and open.
- An ability to frame behaviours and attitudes of client using non-pejorative language.
- A sense of humour.
- An ability to be flexible and inventive.
- Knowing when to say you could be mistaken and openness to correction.

- Promoting an experimental, problem-solving attitude in therapy.
- Being accepting and not judgemental about the client, even when giving or getting difficult feedback.
- Knowing how to give constructive criticism.
- An ability to be firm and to set limits on anti-therapeutic behaviours and attitudes whilst remaining collaborative.
- Sensitivity to negative feelings from clients and oneself and an ability to discuss these relationship difficulties objectively with a colleague or supervisor.
- Therapists, like clients, will have their 'bad or off days' and times when they may be under personal stress. At these times, therapists may find themselves less tolerant and supportive of their clients. Therapists and their supervisors should be aware of these difficulties and approach them in a problem-solving and helpful manner which will optimize the therapist's ability to carry out therapy.

Core beliefs are the automatic thoughts in personality disorder!

In cognitive therapy for clinical disorders, one of the main tasks of cognitive therapy is eliciting and modifying automatic thoughts. In depression, for example, clients are asked to pay attention to the stream of negative thoughts elicited by situations, mental images or memories which result in or arise from dysphoric mood states. In depression, there is an increase in negative automatic thoughts about the self, the world and the future which are the end product of systematic distortions in the way information is processed. In cognitive therapy for personality disorders, the main cognitive task is identifying the key dysfunctional core beliefs and modifying these so that they become more adaptive, less rigid and less absolute. Dysfunctional core beliefs in personality disorder are manifestations of stable underlying unconscious cognitive structures. Information from the environment is integrated into meaningful configurations through schematic structures. In personality disorders, dysfunctional schemas are thought to have arisen in childhood and are assumed to be hypervalent in that they are likely to inhibit or dominate more functional schemas and, are activated in a wide variety of situations, resulting in a consistent bias in the interpretation and meaning of events.

It is the persistent bias in the interpretation of events, whether these be interpersonal, situational, memories or mental images, which needs modification in personality disorders. In therapy, the core dysfunctional beliefs in personality disorders are the main cognitive data set which the therapist seeks to modify. These dysfunctional core beliefs concern central concepts about self and others. Changing core beliefs requires the collection of data that can be evaluated in the light of a modified belief or an alternative more adaptive, less rigid belief. The therapist's task is to lead an examination of the adaptiveness of the old core belief in the client's current life and, through a collaborative process, develop a new, more adaptive belief or modify a pre-existing belief. Then, through Socratic questioning, data that was previously ignored, negated or distorted can be judged by the client for its degree of fit with the new modified belief.

The importance of behavioural change

Individuals with personality disorders are seen as having developed self-defeating behavioural patterns that are overdeveloped to the detriment of other patterns of behaviour which are underdeveloped (Beck *et al.*, 1990). Within the cognitive model, these patterns of behaviours are thought of as being a product of learning to cope and adapt to persistent dysfunctional early experiences with important others such as family members and peers. Schema-driven behavioural patterns may have been adaptive in a child's early environment, but as the child develops and enters into other relationships and explores different environments, those behaviours become self-defeating and dysfunctional. Behavioural, cognitive and affective patterns are thought to be reinforced through the processes of schema maintenance, compensation and avoidance (Young, 1990). Behaviours which are self-defeating and maintain dysfunctional cognitive schemas therefore need to be changed. In order to achieve this, therapy has to focus explicitly on identifying and modifying behavioural strategies which are not adaptive and which are self-defeating. As a result, therapists need to be skilled at utilizing behavioural change strategies as well as cognitive change strategies. As noted in Table 3.1, there is a symbiotic relationship in the treatment of personality disorder between changing schemas and behaviours. Schema changes are unlikely to be achieved or maintained unless the client has also learned to change their behavioural strategies. By using an experimental model of treatment, the client has literally an opportunity to learn and attempt new ways of behaving, to evaluate the impact of new behaviours, and to use the observable data to help in the modification of core beliefs. The main vehicle of change in therapy is the reworking of dysfunctional core beliefs and behavioural patterns.

4

Basic structure and style of cognitive therapy for personality disorders

In order to maintain a collaborative working relationship and keep therapy focused on resolving the client's problems and ameliorating distress, attention needs to be paid to the structure of therapy and to some of the other problems that disrupt the therapeutic relationship. Some of the problems that are reported in carrying out treatment are:

- Non-engagement in treatment.
- Shifting problems and goals.
- Losing focus on the aims of therapy.
- Therapy becomes unstructured as time goes on.
- Non-compliance with assignments.

Length of treatment

Treatment is longer for individuals with personality disorder compared to cognitive therapy for clinical disorders because individuals with personality disorders may have more difficulty engaging in a therapeutic relationship, it will take longer to develop an adequate formulation of the client's long-standing difficulties and to make the necessary changes in habitual and persistent patterns of behaviour and thinking which have developed and been reinforced over years. However, as there is little research in the treatment of clients with specific personality disorders, the question of what is an optimum length of treatment for those with a personality disorder remains largely unanswered. None the less, it is possible for clinically important changes, such as reduction in serious self-harm and improvement in relationships with important others, to be achieved within relatively short time frames of around 18 sessions of cognitive therapy (Davidson and Tyrer, 1996). In practice, it is likely that therapy will take 9 months or more.

Blocking sessions

In order to achieve a structure and focus, treatment can be organized in blocks of sessions which allows for problems to be defined, worked on and outcome assessed. The length of treatment is not left open-ended. From the outset, it is organized into 3-month blocks of at least 10 sessions per block with a review of progress at the end of each block. Problems which the client had stated at the beginning of treatment are reviewed and an assessment is made by both client and therapist of whether or not the initial stated goals have been achieved. On the basis of this information, a new contract will be made for a similar length of time. This would seem to have the advantage of being able to review progress with the option of carrying on or stopping at any 3-month juncture. Given that those with personality disorder can vary in their degree of psychopathology, it is likely that some clients will require more treatment than others and multiple blocks of treatment may be required. However, when progress is no longer evident, treatment should be ended.

This blocking of treatment sessions has three main advantages. First, it provides regular opportunity for both client and therapist to review goals and progress. Secondly, specifying that the treatment will be in 3-month or 10-session blocks prevents both the therapist and client feeling overwhelmed and discouraged by an apparently lengthy treatment. Thirdly, it helps to keep the pace of treatment focused and does not waste time.

Pacing of therapy

The pace of treatment will vary according to the types of problems the client experiences and is attempting to change. Schema change methods require persistence on the part of the therapist and client. Behavioural changes that reinforce schema changes need to be repeated frequently. The therapist therefore needs to be inventive in designing ways of reinforcing behavioural and cognitive changes. Trying to cover too many problems at once is a mistake and suggests that the individual client's problems have not been correctly identified through the shared formulation. Rather, tackling one or two clearly defined problems encourages better collaboration and progress.

Frequency of sessions

Most clients will be seen on a weekly basis at the beginning of therapy to develop a shared formulation which links past and current difficulties. However, as the therapy proceeds, the client will be attempting to make changes which require either data collection or attempting to challenge and change schemas by using either cognitive techniques or trying out new ways of behaving. Collecting evidence that might help modify a core belief may involve several behavioural experiments which are carried out over more than one or two weeks. During such a phase of treatment the client may be seen less frequently but would telephone the therapist in the time between sessions to report progress and as a means of encouraging motivation for change. For example, a client who had a belief concerned with dependency needs thought that she would be unable to cope without the therapist or someone to help her at all times. Treatment sessions were organized with gaps of varying lengths between sessions to test the validity of her assumption that she would not cope without the therapist's help. In between treatment sessions, she was encouraged to carry out tasks for which she would normally have relied on others for help, such as choosing clothes, making a decision about and booking a short holiday and completing an occupational assignment on her own without continuously seeking unnecessary advice and reassurance from colleagues.

As therapy comes to an end, however, sessions are increased in frequency in order to help the client work through any dependency issues which may have arisen within the client–therapist relationship and to concentrate on and work through potential relapse prevention strategies. A separate chapter is included on ending treatment.

Establishing ground rules

The following ground rules are helpful for clients with personality disorders, and to some extent, they mark and define some of the more obvious limits of the client–therapist relationship and the style of therapy which is both open and explicit. It is essential to establish ground rules early in therapy as some clients, particularly those with antisocial tendencies, may seek to find the boundaries of the therapist's patience and tolerance. Having some limits set at the beginning of therapy is helpful in providing a sense of security which then allows a more productive working relationship. To have to set limits, such as those below, later in therapy, is usually the result of a misinterpretation of the therapeutic relationship, and can result in the client feeling chastised and resentful.

Time keeping: therapist and client

The client and therapist are expected to attend appointments on time. If the client is late in attending a treatment session, the session will not be extended in time. It will finish at the time it would originally have been expected to finish. If the client turns up more than half an hour late, the appointment is considered cancelled and a new appointment time agreed.

Missed appointments and cancellations

Reasonable notice of cancellation of appointments should be given by both the client and therapist. In exceptional circumstances, this rule may be violated but it should be emphasized that such circumstances would be rare. The client is expected to take responsibility for missed appointments. If a client misses one appointment, the therapist will send a letter or phone the client offering a further appointment. If a client misses two consecutive appointments, the client is expected to get in touch with the therapist to arrange another appointment and has to provide a realistic explanation to account for the non-attendance and demonstrate in the following sessions that there is a commitment to carry on working. If a client misses three consecutive appointments, the therapy will be considered to have ended. The therapist will write a letter to the client indicating that treatment has ended.

Appointments which are not attended and have not been cancelled by the client, are regarded as having counted towards the total number of sessions of treatment offered. Progress at the end of the pre-arranged number of treatment sessions will therefore be assessed taking into account the missed sessions. This highlights to the client the time-limited nature of therapy and the need for compliance with treatment.

Contact with therapist between sessions

The therapist should not give the client his or her home telephone number or personal address. All clients can contact the therapist by telephoning his/her office in between sessions, but very often, the therapist will be unable to receive the call due to other commitments and may have to contact the client at a later time. No special arrangements need to be made for clients with personality disorders.

If however, some clients are telephoning with greater frequency than others and are attempting to use such calls as a means of increasing therapeutic input, this would become a legitimate item to be discussed in the next face-to-face session with the client.

General outline of treatment sessions

Sessions 1 to 10

Engagement, assessment, formulation and aims of treatment

- Establish rapport and collaboration by being warm and empathic towards the client. The therapist needs to listen carefully to what the client has told them and feedback to the client his or her understanding of the client's problems in a manner which will be perceived as being an accurate understanding of the problems. The therapist should also be explicit about the aims of each session by making a clear agenda with the client.
- If possible, it is helpful to interview someone close to the client, especially as the client's problems are often interpersonal. Those close to the client will often give a clear account of the client's difficulties and how they affect others. This is valuable information for the therapist and for the client. This option has to be presented sensitively to clients and they may need to feel that the therapist is trustworthy and supportive of them before embarking on this strategy.
- Develop an initial formulation of the client's difficulties within the cognitive model. This is shared with the client and should act as a guide to treatment and orients the client to the cognitive model.
- Establish a problem list and agree a priority list which will guide therapy.

Prioritizing problems

As Linehan, in her work with parasuicidal Borderline clients suggests, it is important that suicidal, parasuicidal and life-threatening behaviours should be given priority in treatment (Linehan, 1993a). As this manual is designed to treat a broad range of clients, some of whom will have antisocial traits, any behaviours which endanger or cause harm to others should equally be given a high priority in treatment. Self-damaging behaviour and threatening others with physical violence and acts of aggression warrant being targeted first. These behaviours are always to be given priority over other targets

ORDER OF TREATMENT TASKS

1

Decrease self-destructive behaviours

or

Behaviours which cause harm to others

↓

2

Work on agreed problem behaviours and attitudes

and reduce behaviours and beliefs which disrupt progress in therapy

↓

3

Reinforce schema and behaviour changes

Figure 4.1   Order of treatment tasks

throughout treatment as they have the greatest impact on the individual and those around them.

Following a reduction in the above behaviours, the therapist should then attend to the agreed remaining goals in treatment. These goals should be specified behaviourally if possible so that progress can be easily monitored and the client and therapist are clear about what changes are desired.

The general order in which treatment goals are carried out will be as depicted in Figure 4.1.

Orienting the client to the therapy

In the first 10 sessions, the formulation is used to help the client understand the links between overdeveloped behavioural strategies and underlying dysfunctional core beliefs. The most effective way of putting across the idea of core beliefs is to use the client's own life history and words to illustrate why the client may have come to think and behave in a way that is currently problematic. The handout entitled 'core assumptions' (see Appendix) can be given to the client after the therapist has introduced the idea of core beliefs or schemas. Clients are then introduced to the idea of goal-setting, monitoring behaviour and working with the therapist to acquire the skills necessary to achieve desired goals which will reduce self-defeating behaviours or behaviour which causes harm or distress to others.

Any behavioural, attitudinal or motivational problems which may impede therapy should be dealt with at the time they arise. Problems such as not turning up to appointments or turning up persistently late, not carrying out assignments, changing the agenda of sessions in a haphazard manner or behaving in a hostile manner impede the progress of treatment. These problems require attention and need to be resolved if therapy is to progress in a satisfactory manner.

At the end of the first phase of treatment, the client should have a clear understanding of the development of their problems. It is often helpful to give a client a written account of the formulation and the aims of therapy. As this has been shared with the client and is a summary of what has already been discussed in sessions, the written account of the formulation helps engagement in treatment. Some therapists are reluctant to provide a written formulation, and are concerned that the therapist appears all-knowing. Having shared the formulation and arrived at it through collaboration, this problem is avoided. It is also emphasized that the formulation may change as more information is gathered and a deeper understanding of the client's problems develop.

Session 11 to 20(+)

Aims of second treatment phase: changing core beliefs and maladaptive behaviours

In general, therapy does not move to this next phase unless there is agreement that the client can benefit from working in a structured way, that the goals of therapy are established and there is reduction in self-harm or self-defeating behaviours. If a client is having difficulty reducing self-harm, but is engaged in treatment and shows evidence of being able to work in a structured manner, then the next sessions will continue to focus on self harm or behaviours which cause harm to others.

If appropriate, the therapist and client may wish to continue or increase involvement of significant others in treatment in the second phase of treatment. This can be particularly helpful with clients who have antisocial behaviours and appears to improve compliance with treatment, providing that the therapist remains non-partisan.

The main work of this phase of therapy is however, identifying and weakening core beliefs and working towards new more adaptive beliefs and reinforcing changes in beliefs with a variety of behavioural and cognitive assignments. This work is thorough, repetitive in theme by necessity and requires persistence from both client and therapist.

At the end of the 10 sessions, it is recommended that there is a review of progress. Should this be satisfactory, another block of sessions can be negotiated. Treatment sessions may be spaced out to allow behavioural tasks which reinforce schema change to be carried out.

If clients are socially isolated, it is important to build up constructive contacts and relationships in the client's community. This helps to reduce dependency on the therapist and to increase opportunities to develop other relationships. For some clients this may involve work seeking or at least structured activity of some sort.

Session 30 to 35

The ending phase of treatment

This final phase of treatment is different from the first two phases. The focus here is explicitly on ending therapy and relapse prevention. In order that the client deals with issues of separation and dependency, the frequency of sessions is increased again in this phase to once per week. This allows the therapist to help the client deal with and contain feelings of loss without resorting to self-harming or defeating behaviours or behavioural or affective avoidance.

Over the course of treatment, the client will have been working on developing an array of strategies to aid self-care or improve the quality of relationships. These new strategies have been reinforced through treatment and provide the basis for relapse prevention. Documenting these during therapy as well as providing a list of 'first aid' and longer-term behavioural and cognitive strategies is useful in this final phase.

Maintaining a working alliance

Some of the difficulties which can arise in carrying out treatment with individuals with personality disorders were noted at the beginning of the chapter. In order to encourage and maintain a working alliance and compliance with treatment some other difficulties need to be recognized.

Keep structured and active

Cognitive therapy applied to clinical disorders such as anxiety and depression is a short-term focused treatment. Many therapists treating clients with personality disorder who require longer-term therapy have a tendency to be less structured and focused. The opposite is required: there is a need to remain more problem-oriented and structured with clients with personality disorder. By doing so, the therapist and the client are less likely to become discouraged and are more likely to develop a better therapeutic relationship as well as both being clear about the aim of therapy and the desired outcomes.

Many clients with personality disorders will have had prior experience, not necessarily positive, with mental health service professionals. In order to build up a positive therapeutic relationship, the client needs to feel secure within the relationship. The therapist has to convey a non-judgemental attitude towards the client. This attitude will be evident in the therapist's respect for the client as an individual and in the interest conveyed in learning about the client's problems. In addition, the client needs to have a sense of the content of the therapeutic relationship and where the boundaries of this relationship lie. The client needs to know that this relationship is one which will be built on trust and mutual respect. The therapist needs to know that the client has understood the nature of the relationship so that they can work together effectively. In order to aid the establishment of a therapeutic relationship, the therapist can make certain features of the relationship explicit.

The style of sessions

The therapeutic style is one of openness and collaboration. The therapist and client are both expected to contribute to setting an agenda for the session and there is an agreement to work on the most important problems and not to become side-tracked unnecessarily.

If the client or therapist feels that the other is not collaborating, then this becomes an issue within the session or if appropriate, at the next session. In cognitive therapy, clients are asked for feedback about progress of the session and treatment as a whole. As clients may experience interpersonal problems within the therapeutic relationship itself, the therapist has to be particularly sensitive to any disruption in collaboration. Acknowledging that these difficulties occur and the therapist's openness in taking responsibility for these, when appropriate, is often very important in establishing a working relationship. By doing so, the therapist also provides the client with an example of one way of approaching problems of this kind. In addition feedback from the client can be helpful in that it allows plenty of opportunity for the therapist to acknowledge the client's efforts at collaboration and attempting change.

Clients with personality disorders often behave in ways which can be interpreted negatively. They often hold extremely rigid negative beliefs about the behaviour and motives of others and act in ways which confirm some of these beliefs. Understanding the reasons behind such negative attitudes and behaviours can help the therapist use non-pejorative explanations for the client's behaviour.

Assignments

Devising relevant assignments can challenge many therapists. Likewise many clients have difficulty in attempting and completing assignments. A key to successful learning is that assignments be directly and explicitly related to the client's problems. This will also facilitate the likelihood of compliance. Nevertheless, a commitment to undertaking assignments as a means of extending the influence of the therapy in between sessions and to challenge maladaptive beliefs and behaviour is highly desirable and to be encouraged by the therapist. The onus is on the therapist to be inventive in drawing up useful and relevant assignments and thinking of ways to motivate the client to take part in these. Clients are encouraged in this endeavour if therapists pay a great deal of attention to setting up assignments and to the outcome of these as this reinforces the idea that assignments are an important and integral part of treatment.

Provide a written account of sessions

After a particularly helpful session of cognitive therapy and routinely after a group of sessions, the therapist may give the client a written account of what was learned and achieved. This account is not a verbatim account but a summary of what went on in the session with an emphasis on helping clients to understand their problems within a cognitive therapy framework. This account will often finish with a rationale for behavioural or cognitive assignments and a description of any task agreed by the therapist and client. These accounts are useful in aiding collaboration as they serve a checking function for both therapist and client.

Example of account of session

March 7th
For Susan: my account of our 5th and 6th sessions

We discussed how your father reacted to you when you were not doing well at school. He appeared to lose all interest in you and then when you got into trouble with the police, he told you he wanted no more to do with you. This made you feel unwanted and all alone in the world. You believe that he hated you. From that time, you think that you began to feel very angry and hated everyone. You said that your behaviour got worse and that you got into fights because you did not care if you got hurt and as you disliked other people so intensely at this time, you thought they deserved to get hurt. You thought that there was nobody you could trust to not hurt you.

You now think that your behaviour served to protect you from getting hurt by others as you behaved in a manner which kept others at bay. You now think that your behaviour may not only have kept others away but may also have made other people lose interest in you as you made it so difficult for them to get close to you. This may be why you felt so lonely and abandoned. You think that your behaviour now serves a purpose in that it stops you getting close to people and this then prevents you from taking the risk of getting hurt. You described this strategy as 'I'll hurt them before they hurt me'.

In the second half of the session we looked at your past to find out if you had ever been close to people or trusted people and not been hurt.

(We looked at the evidence for this belief, remembering that you tended to have ignored evidence in the past. Is it possible that you have got close to someone and not been hurt?)

You found it very hard to think of anyone. You did however remember that your Granny had been very nice to you when you were very young. Sadly, she died when you were seven.

Assignment to be carried out this week:

We agreed you would think about the past and see if you could rate the degree to which you trusted the people around you as a child (mother, aunts, uncles, grandparents, brothers and sisters, cousins, teachers, friends).

The exercise that we began in the 6th session suggested that you tend to rate people in an 'all or nothing' way in relation to trust – you tend to place everyone we discussed at the opposite end of trustworthiness. For example, your father was 0% trustworthy. We have included some people who you know now (as an adult) as well as others you knew in your childhood in this exercise to see if you are able to place them on a continuum according to how you judge their level of trustworthiness using your new belief.

Susan's response to this assignment was as follows:

If I trusted someone I would expect them to be prepared to look out for me at least *some* of the time. It is unrealistic to expect this 100% of the time.

Someone whom I trust will not deliberately harm me, either emotionally or physically (see Figure 4.2, Susan's continuum).

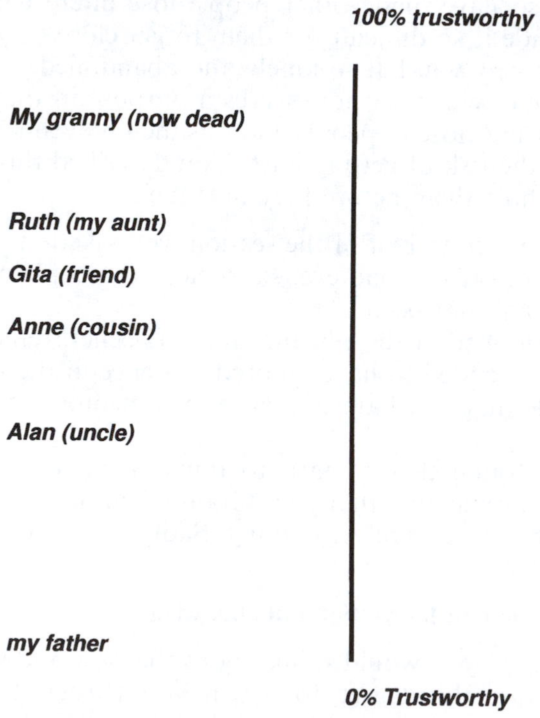

100% trustworthy

My granny (now dead)

Ruth (my aunt)

Gita (friend)

Anne (cousin)

Alan (uncle)

my father

0% Trustworthy

Figure 4.2 Susan's continuum

Supervision

Although the principle of supervision of treatment cases by colleagues and those more expert is regarded as being good practice, it is seldom formalized beyond training years. In the treatment of personality disorder, supervision can be regarded as an important element in treatment. First, this helps to prevent therapy drifting and losing structure and helps to anchor therapy in problem-solving mode. Secondly, it can help the therapist in dealing with negative feelings toward the client which may arise at times. Supervision can encourage the therapist to be realistic about what can be achieved in treatment as well as encouraging the therapist to carry on when setbacks occur. It also helps to stop therapists getting drawn into making negative assumptions themselves about what is possible in terms of change or from acquiescing with a client's dysfunctional beliefs and behaviour instead of challenging these. Clinical supervision can therefore help to clarify and resolve some of these issues and thus help the therapy to reach a more satisfactory conclusion.

5

Arriving at a formulation

The importance of formulation

Formulation has a central importance within cognitive therapy for personality disorder. It provides the client and therapist with a joint understanding of the client's difficulties both historically and currently and acts as an overall framework to guide treatment.

Initial interview

The first interview is an important initial step in assessing the client's problems and personality difficulties and, as this is the first point of contact, the therapist has to attempt to immediately engage the client in treatment. The general demeanour of the therapist is therefore of relevance and the therapist has to convey warmth and understanding of the client's difficulties from the outset whilst also being aware of the potential difficulties which may arise in the client–therapist relationship. Although an initial interview may aim to cover an assessment of some of the client's presenting problems, the history of these problems, personal history and family history and, lastly, what the client hopes to gain from therapy, this assessment will, in reality, take more than one session. Those with personality disorder will have problems which are complex and long-standing and the assessment of these requires structure as well as thoroughness and it is not possible to hurry this process. The therapist has to be alert to problems which may emerge within the therapeutic relationship that mirror interpersonal difficulties in the client's life. The nature of these problems may only be more clearly understood as therapy develops but it is wise to consider what these may be during the development of an initial formulation. These difficulties draw our attention to potential schisms in the client–therapist relationship which may threaten the viability of therapy if they are not averted or used constructively.

Ask a close friend or relative to attend

After the therapist has established that the client's problems might meet diagnostic criteria for personality disorder (for example, ICD-10; Health Organization, 1992a,b) and a formal method of assessment has been carried out, it may be useful to ask the client's permission to interview someone who knows them well, such as a close friend or relative. This suggestion is sometimes resisted initially but once therapy is under way and the therapist has gained the client's trust, the therapist can, once again, ask if the client would agree to someone who knows them well being interviewed. The rationale for interviewing a person well known to the client is that individuals with personality difficulties have interpersonal problems which are directly experienced by those who know them well and therapists can gain a greater understanding of these problems by interviewing a significant other. Clinical experience suggests that significant others are usually particularly willing to come and talk to the therapist and regard the client entering therapy positively as it signifies a willingness to explore changing behavioural patterns and attitudes which interfere with the quality of their relationship.

A friend or relative can often be very helpful in providing additional information about the client's difficulties and the therapist can ascertain the nature and extent of the problems identified by both the client and the accompanying person. Long-standing difficulties can be highlighted as well as more recent problems.

Aims of interview

One of the main aims of the first phase of therapy is to reach a satisfactory formulation of the client's problems and establish the client's diagnosis. This is achieved by finding out what the client's problems are and placing these in the context of the client's personal and family history. Past contact with psychiatric services should give additional information about the history of problems. In addition, interviewing a close relative or friend is helpful in establishing more precisely the nature of problems and whether the problems are of a long-standing nature or represent a more recent change in the client's functioning. One particular difficulty of assessing clients within a mental health setting is that the client may have been referred in an acute phase of a psychiatric disorder and the nature of other difficulties which may be related to personality disturbance are more difficult to establish in such a state. Only after the acute phase of illness has passed can a more reliable assessment of personality disturbance be made and the relative's view and account of difficulties can provide useful information about what are more long-standing traits and problems and what are illness-related problems. By the end of the assessment, the therapist should also have some idea about whether the client would be a suitable candidate for cognitive therapy although it is difficult to predict which clients would respond to cognitive therapy for personality disorder due to lack of available studies in this area. None the less, those patients with personality disorder who suffered from depression in the NIMH collaborative research study of depression had as good an outcome, or did better than, patients without personality disorder, indicating that this form of treatment may well be promising (Shea *et al.*, 1990). From the therapist's point of view, being unable to arrive at an adequate formulation is likely to be a negative indicator for therapy. In terms of patient-related variables, a high degree of avoidance, both in schema activation as well as behaviour, might be a negative predictor as change will be less likely to take place.

Motivation for change

The client's attitude towards the referral and to their problems might be important in establishing their attitude towards any treatment which may follow. For example, a client who disagrees with the referring agent about the nature of their problems is unlikely to begin an interview feeling that they are understood. Clients with personality disorders may not present their problems in the same way as those individuals who have disorders such as depression or obsessive–compulsive disorder. The problems will often be more diffuse and will represent the client's usual functioning as opposed to a change in functioning. As such, the client's distress cannot be necessarily accounted for by a specific change in circumstances or mental functioning. Sometimes clients will have agreed to referral because someone else has thought that they were having difficulties or they were the direct cause of problems for someone else. For example, one client was referred because his wife could not cope with him behaving aggressively towards her. If this client had not come to the first interview (or subsequent interviews) of his own accord, it would have been likely that problems would have arisen in engaging him in therapy. There had to be some advantage to him in turning up for his initial appointment. In his case, the main advantage was to prevent his wife leaving him. He did not, at first, perceive any advantage of changing his behaviour towards her as he believed he had done nothing remarkable in hitting her as other men he knew would have behaved similarly if provoked by their wives. The fact he wanted his wife to remain with him was a starting point for engagement in therapy. It allowed the therapist to help him identify the way his life would be enhanced if he was to improve his relationship with his wife and others and to contemplate changes in his behaviour and thinking which might make him think more highly of himself and others.

History of problems and current difficulties

As the client's history is of relevance to the development of a personality disorder, a general overview of long-standing difficulties and level of functioning is sought. It is, however, important that the initial interviews do not get side-tracked into gathering too detailed an assessment of lifetime functioning and problems. Lifetime functioning is clearly important, but in the assessment phase, only an overview is required. Instead, the client's current problems should be emphasized as these will have brought the client into therapy, and in the case of an individual with a personality disorder, these problems are likely to be representative of their long-standing difficulties.

Establishing rapport

The client's prior experience with health professionals and authority figures may play a part in their attitude towards therapy. A client may have been referred to mental health services before and may well have been told that 'nothing can be done to help'. Helplessness, mixed with frustration and anger, are not uncommon reactions to treatment attempts. Any signs of the therapist being negative, over-whelmed or having difficulty in understanding the client's problems can lead to the client concluding that the treatment will fail and that nothing can indeed be done to help them.

The use of summaries and reflecting back the essence of what the client has communicated helps to establish that the therapist is interested in the client as an individual and has listened carefully and taken their problems seriously. In addition, by summarizing and clarifying the nature of the client's problems, the therapist gives an impression of order and manageability to problems where often there has been little. At all times, the use of non-pejorative language in summaries of the client's difficulties is essential in aiding collaboration and engagement.

Encouraging hope

Many clients with personality disorders will have been seen by other professionals in the past and may have been told that little can be done to help them. Although the therapist cannot offer any easy solutions to their problems, they should encourage the client to think that change is possible. The client and therapist can discuss what changes the client would like to make and how these would be beneficial. If a client is unrealistic about their goals in treatment, the therapist may suggest a more modified goal and seek the client's agreement that this would be acceptable. There is clearly an element of judgement required in deciding what is a 'realistic' goal but if the therapist keeps in mind that the goal of time-limited treatment is to start a change process, then goals can be modified accordingly. Finding a partner, for example, would be an unrealistic goal as the therapist and client have no control over all the factors relating to this endeavour.

However, learning to behave in a more assertive manner or behaving in a friendlier manner would be goals which would be more readily achievable.

The therapist has to encourage the client to have an experimental attitude towards the difficulties they experience. The life-long strategies the client has utilized may not be effective anymore and will have resulted in problems but as these are the only strategies the client has used, the client may not have an idea of both how it is possible to change and what the consequences would be. If the client is sceptical, the therapist should accept this as realistic or even encourage this attitude of scepticism alongside a 'let us try it and see what happens' approach.

Developing a formulation

The cognitive formulation of the client's problems is the foundation of therapy. An adequate formulation will aim to explain the client's symptoms and problems within a particular theoretical framework.

1. Why has the client come for help now?

2. What are the core dysfunctional beliefs?

3. Which emotions/feelings are dominant?

4. What are the overdeveloped and underdeveloped problematic behavioural

   patterns?

5. Are there significant earlier experiences in the client's life which may have

   influenced the development of problematic behaviours and beliefs?

6. How did the client's beliefs become maintained or reinforced?

7. What, if any, are the specific interpersonal problems likely to be

   manifested in the therapeutic relationship and are these typical of

   how the client relates to others?

8. Are there factors in the client's environment which will impede progress

   and change?

9. How will this client respond to cognitive therapy?

Figure 5.1   Developing a case formulation

Without this, therapy will lack direction and the therapist will lack a conceptual framework within which to understand the client and their problems, both past or present. Figure 5.1 outlines questions which aid formulation.

Historical data

The details of the client's life history help in developing an understanding of the nature of the client's long-standing difficulties. Salient childhood and adolescent experiences are likely to be important in the formation of core beliefs about self and others. These experiences may be traumatic but infrequent in nature or have been more repetitive and undramatic, such as having been brought up by neglectful, disinterested parents.

Core beliefs

The cognitive model of personality disorder emphasizes dysfunctional core beliefs which are hypothesized as having had their origin in childhood. The dysfunctional core beliefs concern self and others, and in those with disorders of personality, these beliefs behave similarly to automatic thoughts in that they are observable in the client's narrative. These beliefs are characteristically inflexible and rigid, accepted as truths and phrased in unconditional terms such as 'I am strong' and 'other people are weak'. These beliefs are thought to arise from underlying structures or schemas which are hypervalent and therefore dominant and, as such, more adaptive schemas are less likely to be operational or within conscious awareness. Consequently, the therapist should be able to detect evidence of dysfunctional core beliefs from the client's account of past and present difficulties and from the attitude and behaviour displayed during treatment.

Clients with personality problems may have difficulty in entering into a therapeutic alliance as treatment involves challenging long-held assumptions and core beliefs about themselves and their worlds. Although these core beliefs are dysfunctional, the client's past and present experience has been systematically processed to fit into the core schema. Information which would have weakened the schema has either been distorted to be accommodated into the core schema or ignored.

For many clients with personality difficulties, early negative experiences will have led to the formation of core schemas which may have been adaptive and realistic at one point but become autonomous and unrealistic over time and therefore dysfunctional. In other words, they may indeed have had early experiences which would make sense of the dysfunctional beliefs held in adulthood. However, by behaving in a manner which is consistent with the early core schemas, the schema becomes reinforced rather than weakened and more adaptive schemas are not developed. The personality traits arising from the dysfunctional schemas are therefore also long-standing, rigidly held and pervasive.

The task for the therapist is to actively seek information which would weaken the dysfunctional schemas and allow more adaptive alternative schemas to develop. As the client's dysfunctional schema may have been adaptive at an earlier stage in their life, they will be likely to resist changes to the schema. The client will find change in core schemas threatening and will therefore be resistant or even frightened by the idea that they could change. The functional aspects of personality traits have to be considered as these traits have been long-standing and may, at times, have been of apparent short-term benefit to the client. Ambivalence towards therapy is thus understandable.

For example, a woman who was fostered out as a 6-month-old baby and who had a core belief concerning worthlessness and abandonment had evidence of abandonment in early childhood and of receiving little affection and nurturance from adults due to having subsequently being cared for in children's homes. In adolescence and adulthood, she continued to view herself as being inherently bad and undeserving of affection and love and believed that those whom she got close to would leave her. She developed behavioural strategies related to her core beliefs: she avoided being on her own and would form over-dependent relationships with others but, as she believed she was bad, in adolescence and adulthood, she would frequently act to disrupt and test out these relationships, which led ultimately to others rejecting her. It appeared that schema compensation and schema maintenance were the processes operating to reinforce her behavioural strategies and core beliefs. In therapy, changing her behaviour was anxiety arousing for her as she both risked being independent and more autonomous, and being liked by others at the same time, two conditions she had not believed possible at the beginning of therapy.

Emotions

Those with Borderline personality disorder may have severe difficulties in being able to regulate affect and consequently may show great instability in both the range and intensity of emotions expressed. This can lead to feeling overwhelmed by emotions such as depression or anger and to feeling misunderstood and alone. Such emotional instability can lead the client to a sense of helplessness and hopelessness.

Some clients may speak of their difficulties in an emotionally detached manner. Such blocking of feelings is not uncommon and can often be considered as understandable given the personal history which the client presents. Often clients will have had experiences in childhood that encouraged the suppression of emotions, or they may never have had the experience of having their emotions being taken seriously by adults. For example, being told repeatedly that you could *not* be unhappy by a parent (when you clearly feel unhappy) is likely to invalidate the experience of feeling sad or upset. Clients whose emotional needs have been ignored or unrecognized by others are likely to be unable to express emotions appropriately or to recognize the functional nature of emotions.

Behavioural problems

The cognitive model of personality disorders would predict that when core dysfunctional beliefs are activated, behavioural problems are likely to be evident. As the core schemas are activated across a wide variety of situations, manifested by the persistence of problems, behavioural problems may be evident in many areas of psychosocial functioning.

Behavioural strategies which are overdeveloped and maladaptive in that they undermine the client's ability to lead a more satisfactory life are of prime importance as targets of change in therapy. Both the therapist and the client need to be absolutely clear about which behaviours are to be considered as the focus of treatment. Suicidal, and self-harmful behaviours, if present, should always be a focus of treatment and this should be made clear to the client. Should the client not wish to change those behaviours which are clearly life-threatening, the therapist has a duty to offer or facilitate entry into an alternative treatment, such as admission to hospital, and out-client therapy should not proceed.

This does not imply that clients in treatment will not behave in ways which are self-destructive. The point is that the therapist has to be sure that the client wants to stop behaving in a way that is self-destructive. Clients may, from time to time, feel hopeless and behave in ways which are self-destructive, if not necessarily, life-threatening. None the less, providing that the client in general has a desire to live and to optimize functioning, the therapist can engage the client in attempting to overcome such behaviour. Again the therapist should make clear that he or she is making the assumption that the client wants to improve the quality of their lives and has a desire to work on the problems which they experience.

Occasionally, some of the client's core assumptions may be activated within the therapeutic relationship. For example, one client who assumed that people were always ready to put him down and to interfere with his right to do as he wanted interpreted the therapist's suggestion that he should cooperate with social workers involved with his family as indicating that the therapist was also against him. The therapist needs to be aware of this possibility as it leads to an impasse in treatment if it is not dealt with at the time when it arises.

The client's environment

The client's everyday milieu can also be a potential barrier in treatment. The therapist has to be cautious in assuming that they understand the client's background and current milieu as it may be outside of their own direct experience. Criminal activity, early severe emotional and physical deprivation and abuse and extreme poverty can be comprehended by a therapist but they should guard against making assumptions based on their own (potentially) more limited direct or vicarious experience.

Some clients are likely to have reading and writing difficulties. The therapist should enquire about possible problems in these areas if clients have poor school attendance records or have not achieved scholastically. As well as being a source of confusion and frustration for an individual, literacy problems can hinder therapy if the therapist is unaware that such difficulties exist. Using appropriate language and adapting written materials to the level of comprehension of the client is essential. Encouraging the client to attend adult literacy classes may be highly appropriate and worthwhile in helping them to cope more easily with the outside world.

Discussing the formulation with the client

Around the middle of the first phase of therapy, once the therapist has developed a coherent enough understanding of the client's problems and history, the client should be introduced to the cognitive model of treatment through the formulation. From this framework, the goals and treatment strategies will emerge.

> ### *Example of a formulation*
>
> One client (Jane) stated at the very first session that she was a failure in all areas of her life. Her explanation for her global sense of failure was that she was unlovable and was not worthy of anything good happening to her. Even when things seemed to be going well for her, she said that this

would be by chance and she would manage to make a mess of things by being unable to see things through. When questioned about this further, Jane said that she had always felt unloved and incompetent. Her parents had never believed that she would be able to do well at school. She said that her parents had wanted her to leave school early and get a job. She was the second youngest child in a family of four. She believed that her parents had wanted a baby boy when she was born. Her only brother had died in a car accident and her sisters were, in her view, more attractive, socially skilled and extrovert than she. Her parents had mourned the death of their son and their home contained many reminders of him such as photographs and momentos. As children, her sisters had seemed close to one another and had not wanted her company as she was much younger than them. Her family had been regarded as a 'problem family' in the neighbourhood where she grew up and as a result, the school teachers, neighbours and youth leaders with whom she had come in contact had also regarded her as a problem and no one had ever taken her seriously as an individual. Formal assessment revealed a diagnosis of Borderline personality disorder. A schematic formulation of the problems which she presented is illustrated in Table 5.1.

The therapist used this example to illustrate how a dysfunctional core belief might arise and operate and how cognitive therapy might change this.

Example: Extract from therapy

Therapist: From what you have told me, your experience in childhood gave you a strong message that you were 'no good'. Right from the start you believed that parents did not want you, they wanted a boy. Your sisters seemed to have been close to each other and you felt excluded by them. Your brother died and your parents, who appear to have regarded him as special, have kept his memory alive. All this has made you feel alone and unwanted in this family. At times, even as a child you wished that you could escape from your family. Sometimes you wanted to die, like your brother, in the hope that your parents would be sad about you and show that they cared. No one seemed to be interested in you as an individual. No one believed that you could do anything

Table 5.1   Schematic formulation of Jane's problems

Childhood environment	Never felt you were wanted. Left out on your own, felt unloved Parental mourning over your brother's death
Behavioural/interpersonal	Self-defeating behaviour Stops going to work and is dismissed; avoids contact with others, even friends; over-eats and puts on weight; drinks alcohol to excess on occasions; visits parents when feeling low and ends up feeling worse than before Self-harm (cuts and scratches arms and legs) Three serious overdoses of antidepressants in past (one recently)
Cognitive	
View of self	I am no good I don't deserve things to go right
View of others	Nobody could ever love me Other people can see how bad I am.
Affective	Low mood, anger, shame Emotions are overwhelming at times Feels nothing at times
Motivational	Wish to escape
Action	Avoidance of others or self-punishment
Self-regulatory	Inhibit other-related behaviours

with your life, not even school teachers. It makes sense, given this background, that you felt you were unloved, unwanted and you still have difficulty believing that you will achieve anything in your life. As a child you developed ways of behaving which may have helped you survive in this family. I don't know much about these yet but from what you have told me you became quite withdrawn and quiet so as not to draw any negative attention to yourself. At times you tried to block out your feelings as a way of not feeling depressed.

Some of these behaviours and beliefs about yourself have remained. They made sense when you were a child but now they do not seem to be working in a positive way for you. It seems that you often feel low and angry and sometimes feel so overwhelmed that you want to harm yourself. Cognitive therapy might help you to deal with some of these problems. It works by helping you to become more aware of how you think and feel about yourself and other people and to assess if these old patterns of thinking and behaviour are still appropriate as an adult. Together we can assess if these old ways of thinking, feeling and behaving are the most effective ways for you to get out of life what you want. It also can help you change some of the ways in which you cope with other people. For example, it does not seem to help you to see your parents when you are feeling low but it does help if you go into town shopping. When you are on your own you often dwell on the belief that you are 'no good' and that you are all alone in the world and this seems to lead to you wanting to hurt yourself. Cognitive therapy is about doing what works best for you and learning new ways of behaving and thinking.

The therapist's provisional formulation of the client's problems should be conveyed to the client at an appropriate point in the first phase of treatment. The formulation should be presented as the way in which the therapist has made sense of what is happening in the client's life, past and present.

Focus on identifying core beliefs

Cognitive techniques for other disorders focus on identifying and modifying automatic thoughts and dysfunctional conditional 'if ... , then ...' assumptions. In the treatment of personality disorder, the focus of techniques is at the structural level of core beliefs. These are the unconditional beliefs about self and others.

Explaining core beliefs to clients

Greenberger and Padesky (1995) use a gardening metaphor to explain automatic thoughts, assumptions and core beliefs to clients. For example, a therapist might describe automatic thoughts to be like the weeds and flowers in the garden. Dysfunctional thought records and behavioural experiments are the tools which help an individual to cut down the weeds to ground level to make room for the flowers. However, there are some weeds which are more persistent and which keep popping up again, getting in the way of the flowers. These weeds need to be tackled at their roots, underground. These roots are likened to assumptions and core beliefs and need different techniques and methods to be able to deal with them effectively. These assumptions and core beliefs have taken longer to develop and are more firmly embedded.

Assumptions and core beliefs are not always obvious to us but can be inferred by our actions. Assumptions are sometimes thought of as 'If ... then ...' statements and are less rigid and inflexible than core beliefs. For example, Susan held the following assumption: 'If I can be really nice to other people and do what they want, then they will like me.' In therapy, she was able to modify her assumption through examining the advantages and disadvantages of trying to please others and by testing out an alternative assumption behaviourally, such as asking friends to do something she wanted to do rather than always agreeing to do what they wanted.

Core beliefs are regarded as originating in early childhood and are unconditional statements about self and others. They act like strict rules which we have over-learned and over-obey and we cannot discern when the rule might be wrong. What we learn as children may not always apply to our lives as adults. For example, Margaret, whose childhood was characterized by emotional and physical cruelty, held a core belief that she was 'bad' and deserved to be punished. As a child she made sense of being physically beaten and shouted at by assuming that she had done something wrong. Her reasoning was that she must be bad to deserve so much punishment. From her viewpoint as a young child, adults did not behave cruelly towards others without good reason. As a child, it did not occur to her to question her parent's behaviour towards her. As a result, her core belief was strengthened and her behaviour changed as she became increasingly lacking in confidence and found it hard to try new activities or make friends as others would also know she was bad. As an adult, she continued to believe she was 'bad' and suffered from low esteem and episodes of depression and self-harm. She was also afraid of letting others close to her as they would find out how bad she really was and as a result, she was socially isolated. In addition, she had never tried to find work because she thought she would inevitably fail to do anything properly and be punished. In therapy, this core belief had to be modified by strengthening a competing new belief that she was 'okay' as a person and by keeping records of her behaviour which provided evidence in favour of this new belief. Changing core beliefs takes persistence as the old belief is often taken as being an absolute truth.

Table 6.1 gives some examples of possible core beliefs that are likely to be particularly associated with specific personality disorders. Individuals with personality disorders accept these core beliefs as though they were *a priori* truths. As these beliefs have developed over a lifetime and are held rigidly, they are resistant to change (Young, 1990). The aim of cognitive therapy for personality disorders is to weaken maladaptive core beliefs and strengthen alternative, more adaptive beliefs.

Table 6.1 Examples of core beliefs associated with selected personality disorders

Personality disorder	Core belief
Borderline	I am worthless
Antisocial	Others should serve my needs
Narcissistic	I am a special person
Dependent	I need to have others look after me
Paranoid	I must be vigilant about others at all times

Identifying maladaptive core beliefs

In many ways, the main difficulty for the cognitive therapist is not in identifying core beliefs but in weakening the degree to which these beliefs are held and in strengthening new alternative beliefs. Core beliefs are thought of as originating in early childhood and are unconditional statements about self and others.

Follow the affect

Core beliefs are associated with strong affective responses. Christine Padesky (1994) has suggested that 'following the affect' can help the therapist to identify the content of a schema. She suggests that asking 'what does this say about you?' when a client is upset about an external or internal event, asking 'what does this say about other people?' when someone is distressed about other people, and asking 'what does this say about your life or how the world operates?' can be helpful in accessing self, other and world schemas.

As cognitive, affective, behavioural and other types of schemas are interconnected, modification of one schema will be likely to affect a change in others. In cognitive therapy for personality disorder, the emphasis is on the modification of core beliefs and behaviour and with changes in these, there will be modulation of the affective response that is associated with these schemas.

Methods of accessing core beliefs

Methods that can be used to access core beliefs are:

- Ascertaining the meaning of events which are causing high levels of distress.
- Events within the therapeutic relationship.

- Imagery techniques.
- Exploration of memories, childhood experiences, dreams and daydreams.
- Dysfunctional thought and core belief records.
- Behavioural problems/difficulties.
- Reading relevant books or literature, watching films.
- Self-rating questionnaires.

1 The meaning of events

In the course of therapy, clients report events, either in the past or present, which result in high levels of distress or intense emotional reactions. These reports come through verbal discourse about events and through written homework assignments. The therapist may also observe that the client appears distressed during sessions or appears ill at ease. By asking about the meaning of events which appear to be distressing to the client, the therapist can gain access to themes which directly relate to core maladaptive beliefs.

For example, Patricia had been describing her family life during childhood. She had described how her parents often fought with each other and how she was briefly taken into care at the age of 11 after her mother had died in an accident. Although it may seem obvious to anyone that these events would be distressing, the meaning of the events for the client needs to be established.

Th: Which part of your childhood do you think was the worst? (*direct question*)

P: It was all pretty bad but the bit where my mother left me and my granny told the social services that she couldn't look after me and they put me in a home (*i.e. children's home*).

Th: Do you remember how you felt then?

P: I just remember being very upset and confused.

Th: What did it say about you when your mother left you and your Granny said she could not look after you?

P: Nobody wanted me. I was a 'nobody' that everyone wanted to be rid of.

Th: Is this still how you feel – unwanted by everyone? (*inductive question*)

P: Yes (*looks away, tearful*)

Th: I can see that this must be a very distressing thought. (*therapist validates feelings*) I wonder what it is about being unwanted by everyone that *you* find so terrible?

P: I don't exist – I'm nothing. I must be because everyone just left me – as if I didn't exist.

Th: That seems to be two strong beliefs – that you are unwanted and that you don't exist to others.

P: (*Looks at therapist and nods head*)

Th: (*Therapist tries to link beliefs with past events and current behaviour*) I remember that you told me something like this when you want to cut yourself? (*Client nods*) Are there other times which you can identify thinking like this?

P: I have always thought that no one wants me. If anyone ignores me, I feel like I don't exist. I'm not important to anyone and no one cares about me. That's the way I think.

2 Events within the therapeutic relationship

Clients with personality disorders have problems in relationships with other people which manifest themselves within the therapeutic relationship. It is essential the relationship with the therapist be regarded as a microcosm of all relationships within which difficulties can be safely assessed and resolutions attempted. The therapeutic relationship is an ideal vehicle for an individual to test out whether their assumptions about others are true and to learn the impact of their behaviour on others.

Mood changes within the session, physical or verbal reactions to what the therapist does or says, are all cues to maladaptive core beliefs. The therapist can encourage the client to test the reality of their beliefs directly in the client–therapist laboratory.

For example, one male client (with a dependent personality disorder and depressive disorder) attempted to delay the departure of the therapist on holiday by refusing to leave the therapist's office at the end of a treatment session. He began to cry and stamp his feet in anger. The therapist initially acknowledged that he was distressed but did not draw attention to his angry behaviour (as this was regarded as probably being secondary to the activation of his primary core belief that the therapist was abandoning him) and asked what did it mean to him that the session had come to an end and she was going on holiday. He said that she did not like him and was leaving him at a crucial stage in treatment because he was so awful and she did not care what happened to him. His core belief was that he was helpless. Consequently, he was afraid that others would abandon him particularly when he was in great need.

3 Imagery techniques

From the client's account of their life history and specific memories, the therapist will have some idea about the nature and content of core beliefs. By choosing an incident which appears to be significantly upsetting to the client, the therapist can help the client to increase the vividness of recall and by doing so, may trigger a core schema and access the core belief. The therapist asks the client to close their eyes and report the scene in detail: where the incident took place, who was there and what happened. It is more powerful to have the incident described in the present tense and using the first person. It is particularly important that the client experiences some of the affect connected with the incident. Once this has been recalled vividly, the therapist can ascertain the meaning of reported event.

Some clients may try to distance themselves from events which are upsetting (schema avoidance), describing the incident in an overly general and superficial manner. Encouraging the client to recall the incident by trying to feel their way into the scene and increasing the level of descriptive information can be helpful. Asking the client how they are feeling as they describe the incident, cues the client to recall the associated affect. This way the client will be more likely to recall the incident with greater accuracy and vividness.

4 Exploration of memories, childhood experiences, dreams and daydreams

As schemas are formed in early childhood, focusing on the client's childhood experiences will help to identify maladaptive core beliefs. Asking the client to highlight the happiest and the most upsetting memories of childhood focuses the therapist and client to select relevant events.

Memories which are connected with high emotional tone from any stage of development are likely to be useful in identifying maladaptive beliefs. Ask the client to identify these memories and discuss them within sessions.

Daydreams can be regarded as 'what if' fantasies. Asking the client to actively daydream and report how they would wish their world and important relationships to be can help to point to underlying core beliefs. For example, a client with an Antisocial personality disorder fantasized that others would ask him for advice and that he would be able to have power and influence over the lives of others. When asked if this was how he usually thought, he reported that he was certain he was superior to others in many aspects but when asked about how he thought others saw him, he acknowledged he had difficulty getting others to recognize his superiority. At work, he had frequent disagreements with other men about issues to do with work practices and about opinions on matters in the current news. He regarded his workmates as stupid and dismissed their opinions, alienating himself from them.

5 Dysfunctional thoughts and core belief records

The records of automatic thoughts commonly used in the treatment of Axis I disorders can also be useful in a modified form in the treatment of personality disorder. The forms can be used to record examples in the client's current life when a schema is active. For example, one client kept a record of the type of situation in which she felt that other people were rejecting or humiliating her (see Figure 6.1). This allowed the client and therapist to assess the impact of her core belief and was helpful in convincing the client that her belief operated in a variety of settings and that it may not have always been adaptive.

6 Behavioural problems or difficulties

Behavioural problems, often in the form of difficulties with other people, are a hallmark of personality disorders. Specific avoidance of certain behaviours also may point to underlying core beliefs. Some case examples are described below.

State belief: Other people will try to humiliate and ridicule me

Degree to which you believe this to be true: 99%

Situation	Degree to which belief is accurate	How did you react?
Woman at bus stop pushed in front of me	95%	I made a scene
The gas meter reader did not turn up to read my meter	95%	I phoned the company and got angry. They put the phone down on me
My sister told me I was getting fatter	100%	I hit her and told her she was not so wonderful herself

Figure 6.1 Record to identify the impact of my core belief

Graham

Graham is a 22-year-old man (Avoidant personality disorder) who was referred for treatment by his General Practitioner for treatment of his anxiety symptoms. The referral letter contained very little information other than he had reported feeling very anxious in social situations and this was having an impact on his finding a job, although he had reasonable passes in school qualifications. Part of the initial assessment of Graham's problems involved obtaining information about his pattern of relating to other people. Graham was initially reluctant to provide much information on this topic. He sat, twisted round in the chair looking out the window, or would hold a tissue to his nose for long spells, making communication difficult and awkward. He stated that he had not had the opportunity to develop friendships but could not explain why he had not had this chance. After several sessions in which the therapist had been non-confrontational but interested in finding out more about his problems, he began to give the therapist more information about his problems with others. He described patterns of behaviour which suggested he was very guarded with others and tended not to get involved with other people. He had no friends and spent his time alone. He was afraid of applying for jobs or courses for two main reasons: he may be turned down and secondly, if he did get an interview or a job, he could not face being with other people in a situation where his performance would be scrutinized. He described childhood behavioural problems such as refusing to play with others, avoiding sports at school and having been bullied at one of the primary schools he attended. His parents had been strict with him as a child and had not allowed him to play with children who lived around his home as they had regarded these children as being too rough. Although his parents had never explicitly said as much, Graham had always had the impression that he was not the clever and talented son that they had wished for and was really not good enough. They had been lukewarm about his school performance and only if he had been in the top 10% of the class, had they been enthusiastic about his performance. His lack of sportsmanship had been a source of disappointment to his father, who was a keen golfer. As an adolescent, he had been terrified of speaking to girls and remembered being teased by girls at his school when he had no one to sit beside in science classes. He had been very afraid of blushing or stammering if asked a question by a teacher and had skipped classes successfully without being caught.

From Graham's account of some of his childhood and adolescent experiences, it appeared he was afraid of showing signs of anxiety or social discomfort to others. His initial reluctance to speak to the therapist and to apply for courses or work suggested that he was overly sensitive to signs of disapproval from others and could be easily hurt. Although there was evidence that he was at least of above average intelligence, he had under-achieved both at school through avoidance of classes, and as an adult through not applying for further education courses or appropriate work. His past and present behaviour suggested an avoidant personality disorder. He held two core beliefs. 'Other people will think I'm peculiar' and 'I'm no good'.

Carol

Carol was a 28-year-old woman who had a diagnosis of Borderline personality disorder who was referred for therapy after an overdose. She had a history of deliberate self-harm, both overdoses and cutting. She also reported several other problematic behaviours such as over-eating when she was alone, taking on too much responsibility for others then being unable to meet her commitments and difficulty establishing regular sleeping habits. These problematic behaviours were each discussed in therapy. From her account, it appeared that she over-ate to avoid negative feelings and thoughts about herself such as 'I am ugly' and 'nobody likes me'. By stuffing herself with food, she became less aware of her thoughts and surroundings and more focused on eating, thus at least temporarily blocking out her negative feelings and negative view of herself. It was obvious that this was not an adaptive behaviour as she would eventually become very distressed by bingeing and believed that she was disgusting and would never be liked or accepted by others. Her self-harm behaviour was similar in that it initially blocked out her negative feelings and self-view but only temporarily. Taking on too much responsibility for others appeared to be directly related to her desire for others to like her, although she was ambivalent about becoming too close to others as they might reject her when they realized that she was 'no good'. She believed that others would like her if she did things for them. As this was often at her own expense in terms of energy and time, this strategy often back-fired and she was unable to keep her promises of help, thus confirming her belief that she was 'no good' and that others would not like her.

7 Literature and films

One client became so distressed describing her childhood experiences that she suggested to the therapist that she watch a film which she had found deeply upsetting. This allowed the therapist to make links between the female character in the film and the client's childhood. Later the client was able to experience some of the anger and sadness which she had felt at school and at home but without becoming overwhelmed and thinking that she was unable to cope. Various beliefs were uncovered concerned with she was undeserving of happiness of any sort and that vanity in any form was an unforgivable sin.

A male client who had been sexually abused in childhood said he avoided thinking and talking about what the experience meant to him but could not stop being upset about it. The therapist asked if he would be willing to watch a documentary about sexual abuse with the therapist and discuss it afterwards. The very suggestion of doing such a thing increased anxiety in the client and when asked about this, he told the therapist that he thought she would regard him as weak and disgusting and he would feel so ashamed he would not be able to cope (his dominant belief).

8 Self-rating questionnaires

The Dysfunctional Attitude Scale (DAS) (Weissman and Beck, 1978) is a self-report inventory of basic attitudes or beliefs, derived from Beck's (1967) cognitive theory of depression, which are assumed to underlie depressive thinking. The scale contains items which relate to 'if . . . then . . .' assumptions which were collected from clients without personality disorder undergoing treatment. This scale can aid the therapist in determining dominant themes which may then be related to core beliefs such as achievement, love, approval, perfectionism and autonomy.

The Schema Questionnaire (Young and Brown, 1990) is a self-completion questionnaire which contains items that relate to 16 schemas or themes which are thought to be relevant to personality disorder. These are as follows: emotional deprivation, abandonment, mistrust and abuse, social isolation, defectiveness and shame, social undesirability, failure to achieve, functional dependence and incompetence, vulnerability to harm and illness, enmeshment, subjugation, self-sacrifice, emotional inhibition, unrelenting standards, entitlement, insufficient self-control and self-discipline.

These questionnaires are a useful starting point if clients and therapists are having difficulty in assessing schemas. In addition, if used in the assessment phase of treatment, they may provide the therapist with a means of evaluating the degree of change in beliefs as therapy progresses.

7

Focus on changing core beliefs

Cognitive therapists can utilize schema change techniques from standard cognitive therapy to modify dysfunctional assumptions with personality disorders (see Blackburn and Davidson, 1995) but these techniques may not be as effective with core beliefs, which are more rigid and inflexible and believed absolutely. Changing core beliefs in those with personality disorder requires persistence and several different techniques may be required to change the same belief. Clinical experience also suggests that core beliefs will be related to maladaptive behavioural strategies which have to altered in conjunction with strengthening new alternative beliefs.

Christine Padesky (1994) has described the first three of the following change strategies that can be used in therapy (see Figure 7.1). The fourth strategy is used for core beliefs that impinge on interpersonal relationships.

1 Continuum

Clients with personality disorders tend to accept their core beliefs as accurate representations of self and others. Having never questioned or challenged these beliefs, they usually state that they believe a core belief to be absolutely true. They simply accept that the belief is correct. Through schema maintenance, avoidance and compensation processes (Young, 1990), evidence against the schema will have been ignored or distorted to fit the schema in order for the schema to survive. By using guided discovery and questioning the evidence for a core belief, a client can become less rigid in the degree to which they endorse a specific belief.

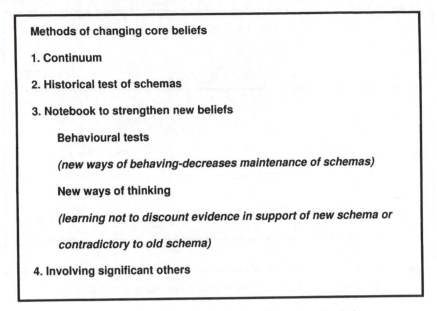

> **Methods of changing core beliefs**
>
> **1. Continuum**
>
> **2. Historical test of schemas**
>
> **3. Notebook to strengthen new beliefs**
>
> > **Behavioural tests**
> >
> > *(new ways of behaving-decreases maintenance of schemas)*
> >
> > **New ways of thinking**
> >
> > *(learning not to discount evidence in support of new schema or*
> >
> > *contradictory to old schema)*
>
> **4. Involving significant others**

Figure 7.1   Methods of changing core beliefs

The therapist can aid the development of alternative beliefs by utilizing various continuum strategies.

The uni-directional continuum

Paula believed that she was 'a total failure'. It was evident from Paula's description of herself that she believed this absolutely and she was able to list many examples of her failure and worthlessness: she had never done well at school and had failed exams, although she made friends with her peers easily, she had always fallen out with these girls, she had been in employment twice since leaving school but both jobs had come to an end and she was currently unemployed.

The therapist decided to use a continuum which ranged from 0% to 100% using alternative beliefs which were 'I am okay as a person' and 'I can succeed in my life' (see Figure 7.2). These alternative beliefs were chosen after discussion with Paula of what she regarded as acceptable in terms of more adaptive beliefs. She was asked to place herself on each of these continua and rated herself 2% on the first and 0% on the second. Through earlier questioning of her belief that she was a failure, she had become aware that she had some evidence that she was an acceptable person. For example, two days before coming to a therapy session she had helped a neighbour to cope with a newly born baby who was crying all the time. Paula had looked after her

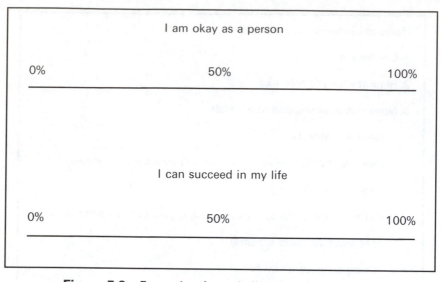

Figure 7.2 Example of a uni-directional continuum

siblings when they were young and had much experience of dealing with babies and small children. However, she had difficulty maintaining this stance as she would either ignore the evidence or tell the therapist that she had not described all the details, and if the therapist knew all the details of her failures, she too would agree that she was a total failure.

Educating Paula on how schemas and core beliefs functioned was helpful in that she became more adept at recognizing how she dismissed or ignored evidence which would have strengthened the new alternative core views of herself as being 'okay' as a person and able to succeed in her life. Developing specific criteria by which Paula could assess her new beliefs was essential as she had difficulty with abstract concepts and would judge herself in very global black and white terms. A key step in this process was getting her to list how she judged other people. They were usually regarded as being happy and much more able to cope and make a success of their lives.

These continua were used in every session of therapy and any examples of her being 'okay' or 'successful' from the days between sessions were recorded and kept in her personal file which she brought to therapy sessions. Those shown in Figure 7.3 were gathered over several sessions. Eventually Paula became more able to recognize events, behaviours or thoughts which fitted her new schemas and was able to record these in her personal file during the intervals between sessions.

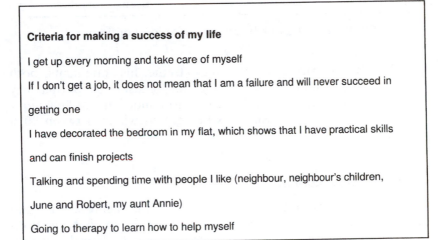

Criteria for being okay as a person

Other people ask for my help and they say I am understanding

I don't have to agree with everyone. My opinions are valid

Everyone has intrinsic worth

I can enjoy myself sometimes and can be sad sometimes and both are normal

Criteria for making a success of my life

I get up every morning and take care of myself

If I don't get a job, it does not mean that I am a failure and will never succeed in

getting one

I have decorated the bedroom in my flat, which shows that I have practical skills

and can finish projects

Talking and spending time with people I like (neighbour, neighbour's children,

June and Robert, my aunt Annie)

Going to therapy to learn how to help myself

Figure 7.3   Paula's criteria for being okay and successful

Throughout therapy the continuum can be used to measure progress in treatment. For example, after several behavioural experiments where a client deliberately did not demand extra attention from the therapist, her friends and relatives, she rated her alternative belief, 'I can survive without the help of others', as 40% as opposed to 0% at the beginning of treatment.

As many clients have idiosyncratic beliefs, the meaning of these may not be transparent. For example, Keith, the dependent young man mentioned earlier, held the belief he was helpless. In order to clarify what he meant by this belief, criteria were developed. He was then able to re-assess and evaluate the degree to which he had been helpless in the past and present. His criterion continuum is set out in

I am helpless

0%	100%

I always complete things on my own	I always ask for help from others

I never travel with other people	I always have to travel with someone else

I spend every moment on my own	I always have other people around me

Figure 7.4   Keith's belief and criterion continuum

Figure 7.4. By polarizing, or making extreme, his statements, both ends of the continuum were clearly not realistic or particularly adaptive. He was able to re-evaluate his more independent behaviour and his belief in his helplessness as being somewhere between 40% and 50%.

Two-dimensional continuum

One client held two inter-related beliefs about achievement and pleasure. He had always worked exceptionally hard in his occupation and had achieved a great deal but over the years he had derived no pleasure from work. One of the main reasons for this lack of pleasure was that he believed he had to achieve in order to have any sense of self-worth. He had not paid attention to other aspects of his life and had devalued anything which was not work-related. Unfortunately, the company he worked for had financial problems and his job had been down-graded. He had taken this personally, felt he was a failure and had subsequently become depressed. He perceived achievement and pleasure as dimensions in his life which were diametrically opposed to one another. By using a two dimensional continuum, the therapist was able to break down his belief that pleasure and achievement were opposites (see Figure 7.5). He was able to place work, other activities and even relationships with his parents and children, on these two dimensions and realized that they were not always opposed to one another. For example, he believed that he had, in his view, a reasonably good relationship with his children which he had been instrumental in developing and which was a source of pleasure to him. As therapy progressed, he was able to add other

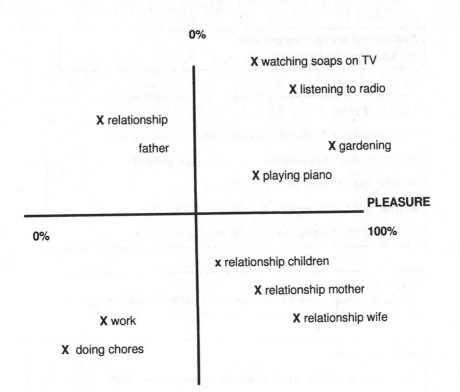

Figure 7.5   Example of a two-dimensional continuum

sources of pleasure which were not achievement oriented such as gardening and playing the piano.

2 Historical test of schemas

As it is assumed that core beliefs develop in childhood and are maintained and reinforced throughout a lifetime, a review of a client's life history can be carried out to test out the validity of a schema. Padesky (1994) recommends that the client and therapist make two lists of evidence, one list supporting the schema and another disconfirming the schema. Suitable developmental time periods are selected such as infancy, early childhood (ages 2–4), early school age (5–10) etc (see Figure 7.6). One of the aims of the historical test of schemas is for the client to become more aware of the positive and

> **Evidence that supports the old belief**
> **Old belief: other people think I am strange**

> **Age 8 to 12 years**
>
> My family lived a very different lifestyle from other families around us
>
> My mother had breast cancer and died when I was 8 years old
>
> My father was a bit weird after my mother died
>
> Both my parents were members of an unusual religious sect
>
> Both sets of grandparents disapproved of my parent's religion

> **Evidence that supports a new belief**
> **New belief: being different from others does not mean I am strange or weird**

> **Age 8 to 12 years**
>
> There were other children at school who lost a parent through death
>
> I played football with other boys
>
> I was always picked for the school choir because I could sing well
>
> Other kids at school had different religions too and I did not think they were strange
>
> I could not do anything about my Mum dying and my Dad being depressed and they could not do anything about this either

Figure 7.6 Example of a historical test of schema

negative experiences they have had over their lifetime and to develop a sense of compassion towards themselves.

Some clients have little information about their early years. One client, John, had a core belief 'I am different' and had severe interpersonal problems. He had no information about his first four years and had no one to ask as his parents were both dead and he was not close to his other relatives. The exercise was none the less useful as he realized how unusual his early life had been and began to understand why he had such difficulties relating to other people and to his own two sons.

John's core belief was that other people thought he was strange and different. This had led to him having problems relating to others whom he thought did not understand him.

John's historical test of schemas took many weeks to complete. Some of the historical test was completed as assignments and some was completed during sessions when evidence became available through discussion of the past or present. At various times during the exercise, John was asked by the therapist what he thought the evidence implied about other people thinking he was weird. Although he had been initially convinced that his belief was 100% correct, later in therapy, he did not believe this to be so. Instead, he saw that some people had been kind and generous to him in the past even though they knew his family may have had different views on religion than his own. Others had been accepting of his sect but had not interfered in any way. He also realized that he had been deprived of loving and caring parents through their deaths and that he had a right to be upset about this. He gathered information about his mother and discovered that she had been seriously ill for almost all his childhood. He stated on several occasions that she had been very brave and stoical about her illness and he had the impression she had always tried to do the best thing for him. As therapy went on, he remembered how some women in the village where he lived would come to the house to help his mother when she must have been ill. He surmised that, unlike his grandparents, they had been accepting of his family's religious beliefs and had not made an issue of this. Whether this was true or not, he at least developed some flexibility in his belief that others saw him as weird. He stopped ignoring and distorting evidence which suggested that other people may be acting in a neutral manner or even behaving in a positive manner towards him.

3 Notebook to strengthen new schema

Another powerful method of changing beliefs is keeping a positive data log (Padesky, 1994). Essentially, this involves the client keeping a data record of all experiences and thoughts which would represent a new adaptive belief. The main change technique here is getting the client to challenge the core belief by learning not to distort or ignore information that would not fit with the core schema. Sylvia had a core belief that she was stupid . She could list numerous examples of her stupidity and no evidence that suggested she was as intelligent as most people. For example, when she re-calculated a gas bill and telephoned the company pointing out their mistake, she was asked by the therapist if this was an example of her behaving 'intelligently'. Paula told the therapist that anyone could have done what she did. Paula ignored or distorted evidence which suggested she behaved intelligently. Even when she conceded to having behaved intelligently, she thought that there was either exceptional circumstances involved or it was just a one off exception.

Like Paula, clients have to learn not to ignore, discount or distort evidence that is contradictory to a core belief. The therapist's role is to keep pointing out examples of schema maintenance. At first, it is as if the client has to learn where to place this information. The therapist has to help the client grasp and hold on to contradictory evidence. Having a notebook to record evidence which does not fit the core belief is essential in building up more adaptive schemas. Sometimes it is easier for the therapist to record this at first and after a few sessions, hand the notebook over to the client to record examples during the days between sessions.

The notebook is useful for recording examples of new ways of behaving as well as new ways of thinking about self and others. It is important that the therapist keeps attending to what is recorded in the notebook so that these new beliefs are reinforced. The notebook literally provides a store for evidence that fits a new belief where previously the client had no schema to record or keep this information (see Figure 7.7 for an example from Paula's notebook).

4 Involving significant others

The client's immediate environment is often a major factor in maintaining schemas or core beliefs. It is possible that partners or family unwittingly reinforce a client's core belief about themselves or others. Sometimes an individual will inadvertently 'choose' relationships that are unhelpful and these relationships then confirm the client's negative self-concept, especially when these relationships are ultimately detrimental.

During treatment, the therapist can assess which relationships serve to maintain a client's negative self-view. Creating an opportunity to work with a significant other to change the client's negative self-view is important in developing a new alternative view of self. Often the therapist will have to work with the significant other as that individual may have also developed a rather rigid view of the client. One way of producing a change in the relationship is to ensure that both individuals benefit from any changes which may take place and that the relationship works better and is more effective than it was before.

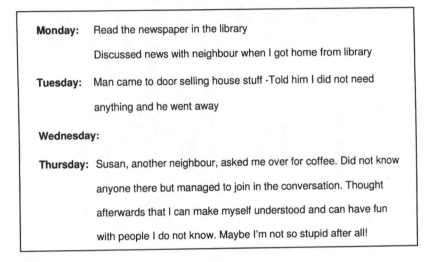

Old belief: I am stupid
New belief: I am as intelligent as most people

Monday: Read the newspaper in the library

Discussed news with neighbour when I got home from library

Tuesday: Man came to door selling house stuff -Told him I did not need

anything and he went away

Wednesday:

Thursday: Susan, another neighbour, asked me over for coffee. Did not know

anyone there but managed to join in the conversation. Thought

afterwards that I can make myself understood and can have fun

with people I do not know. Maybe I'm not so stupid after all!

Figure 7.7   Example from Paula's notebook to strengthen new belief

One client with Borderline personality disorder (Carol) became dependent on her 'foster' sister Mary whom she idealized. Carol believed that she could not cope without Mary's help. Carol had difficulty recognizing that Mary had her own life to lead and would phone Mary at any hour of the day and night. Apparently Mary never complained about this. Mary unwittingly reinforced Carol's idea that she was helpless and could not cope with a crisis, regardless of how small this might be.

A meeting with Mary revealed that Mary was glad to help Carol as she found this satisfied her need to be useful to others. The therapist pointed out that although their relationship with each other was mutually satisfying there were also some drawbacks. Both women were initially rather resistant to the idea that there may be disadvantages in the way they related to one another. However, when the therapist then gave several examples from the experience of other couples, both were able to list some disadvantages. Mary in particular was relieved to be able to discuss her relationship with Carol as she had been finding herself stressed by Carol's phone calls and demands for help. Carol said that she never learnt to cope on her own and that she knew that Mary could not always be available for her. Mary was relieved that she did not have to go on attending to Carol's every need and was able to state that she would be able to use her energies more effectively to help Carol if she was clear that it was a real crisis.

8

Typical behavioural problems: Antisocial personality disorder

This chapter concentrates on some of the more typical behavioural problems presented by clients with Antisocial personality disorder. Some of these problems, for example, alcohol abuse, may be common to more than one type of personality disorder.

As emphasized before, all treatment is guided by the therapist's formulation of the client's problems, and together they decide on which are the most important behavioural problems to concentrate on in treatment. Some problems take priority over others and are primary targets of treatment. For example, problems such as harm to others, if present, would require to be the focus of initial change. Other behavioural problems, which reflect long-term maladaptive behavioural strategies, require that systematic assessment and changes to behaviour are made in conjunction with changes in relevant core beliefs. All change, both at a schematic level and behavioural level, therefore rest on the development of an adequate formulation. Without a formulation, therapy will proceed in piece-meal manner and will lack an overall sense of cohesion.

Antisocial personality disorder

Clients with Antisocial personality disorder have difficulty maintaining stable relationships with others and behave irresponsibly and impulsively. They appear to disregard the feelings of others, have difficulty seeing things from someone else's perspective and tend to blame others, rather than themselves, for things which go wrong. Cognitive therapy for Antisocial personality disorder aims to improve social behaviour and the ability to function in a more morally aware manner by changing the way in which an individual construes himself or herself in relation to others (Beck *et al.*, 1990). Clients with this disorder are regarded as having a developmental delay in moral maturity and cognitive functioning. This group of clients often show intellectual difficulties which have been described, using Piagetian concepts, as a tendency to operate at a concrete rather than abstract level of intellectual functioning. Such individuals will have difficulty taking the perspective of another. They will tend to react to situations in immediate terms without first considering the possible longer-term consequences of their actions. In general, clients with Antisocial personality disorder will lack problem-solving skills as these skills require an ability to reflect on and identify problems and their consequences and to generate potential solutions to problems.

Treatment focus

As with other personality disorders, treatment for Antisocial personality disorder focuses on the client's difficulties in a systematic manner. Treatment tasks are graded in complexity and sophistication according to the cognitive level at which an individual is functioning (Beck *et al.*, 1990). At the most basic level, clients will be solely concerned with self-interest and will be unable to consider the consequences of their actions beyond immediate rewards. The task of the therapist is to attempt to increase the client's ability to consider their actions and to consider the longer-term advantages and disadvantages of behaving in a manner that may be counterproductive. The therapist has to attempt to understand the client's view of themselves and how the client relates to other people. The schemas which underlie such behaviour and cognitive functioning will tend to be rigid and simplistic. Clients with Antisocial personality disorder often believe that they can do exactly what they feel like doing and that other people are there to be used and exploited for their benefit. Any change in attitude from this view or change in behaviour which demonstrates that the individual has considered their actions and the implications such actions may have for self and others has to be reinforced by the therapist. The therapist may assume that the client continues to act out of self-interest but tries to ensure that the client's actions become more functional and adaptive. Clients are systematically reinforced for considering the 'possible' in favour of what is happening in the immediate environment.

Once the client has begun to be able to consider the longer-term consequences of their behaviour, the therapist can attempt to move to

Table 8.1 Examples of targets of behavioural techniques

Problem	Technique
Alcohol abuse	Self-monitoring (e.g. weekly diary)
	Pros and cons of drinking
	Stimulus control
	Finding alternatives to alcohol
Anger	Feelings vs. actions
	Self-monitoring (e.g. frequency count)
	Stimulus control
	Assertiveness training
	Social skills training
Relationship difficulties	Behavioural contracting
	Increasing positive behaviours
Poor literacy skills	Attend adult literacy classes
Poor work record	Graded assignments
	Scheduling work finding

a more advanced level of cognitive functioning. At this level, clients will be able to consider a range of possible options for behaviour and thinking. The client's beliefs about others and self can be explored further at this stage. The idea that the client may not always be right and that other people may be affected by their behaviour may be introduced at this stage. Beliefs such as 'I do what I like because it feels right' and 'other people should see things my way' are examined in terms of their adaptiveness and schema change methods applied.

Interviewing a client's close family member or partner provides useful information on problem behaviours as well as potentially underlining to the client that others are affected by their behaviour. Behaviours which cause harm to self and others are given the highest priority in treatment. Although the therapist may be concerned about the effect of the client's behaviour on others, the focus continues to be centred on the client's behaviour and needs. The therapy attempts to alter the client's dysfunctional behaviour and thinking. Table 8.1 gives some examples of problems which are responsive to behavioural techniques.

Behavioural techniques

Behavioural techniques are used throughout treatment in conjunction with cognitive techniques. Carrying out a functional analysis of

Table 8.2 Example: self-monitoring methods

Self-monitoring method	Examples of targets
Diary keeping	Positive behaviours Alcohol consumption
Activity schedules	Daily activities Recording work
Frequency counts	Feeling angry
Time sampling behaviours	Speak to children Speak (pleasantly) to wife

behavioural problems is an essential first step in being able to attempt a solution. This will provide information on the antecedents, behaviour, and consequences of behaviour. Once a clear picture has emerged of the behaviour, potential solutions can be generated by both therapist and client.

Self-monitoring

Clients with Antisocial personality disorder are usually deficient in self-monitoring skills. Through training in such skills, clients can learn to be more careful observers of their own behaviour and this enhances their ability to be able to stand back and observe themselves as opposed to being egocentrically focused. Training in this skill can be therapeutic in itself, as it can have an indirect effect on the behaviour being monitored. Methods used in self-monitoring and examples of target behaviours are listed in Table 8.2.

The therapist can use several methods to obtain information about specific behaviours. A weekly activity schedule will provide information on all activities and can be useful for building up a picture of the client's daily life. Keeping a diary of specific behaviours can be used for behaviours that are less frequent, such as acts of aggression or, concentrating on more adaptive behaviours, acts that show consideration of others. Frequency counts are useful for recording high frequency events such as feeling angry. Time sampling can also be used for such high frequency behaviours or events.

Alcohol abuse

Alcohol abuse and its consequences often constitute a major problem for this group of clients. Abstinence from alcohol may be an appropriate goal of treatment if an individual is dependent on alcohol, or if the consequences of their alcohol consumption are serious. For example, one client who drank alcohol on very few occasions nevertheless encountered problems of such severity that abstinence was recommended. On consuming alcohol, he usually drank more than he had intended to, and on more than three occasions in the past had become involved in serious physical fights which had led to several charges of assault. For him, although consuming alcohol was a low frequency event, his drinking was a high-risk activity as it often lead to acts of aggression.

Even when alcohol dependence is not present, excessive alcohol consumption may bring about problems in several areas of an individual's life, including mental and physical health, relationships, work and the law. Clients may not recognize the role played by alcohol in generating or maintaining problems in several areas of their lives. They may even deny that alcohol consumption and its consequences could be a problem for them. A careful assessment is required to tease out problems which may be related to the consumption of alcohol.

Self-monitoring in the form of keeping a daily diary gives useful information on quantity and frequency of drinking as well as on the consequences of alcohol consumption. This can provide a baseline measure of the quantity of alcohol consumed which can then be compared with alcohol consumption after a treatment intervention. Clients may sometimes not be aware of the effect or impact of alcohol on their problems and a drinking diary can help to elucidate the relationship between problems and alcohol consumption.

Below is an example of an extract from a drinking diary (see Figure 8.1). From the data available in the extract, the client and therapist deduced that going out earlier in the evening and drinking alcohol in the presence of Bobby and Malcolm may lead to consequences which are undesirable.

For some individuals, reducing alcohol consumption may be a more appropriate goal than abstinence. This is often a more difficult option as it involves sticking to agreed levels of consumption and being vigilant about where and when drinking takes place. For clients who have difficulties in self-monitoring and who do not always believe in the necessity for consistency in their own behaviour, this task may be too difficult at first and the client may resist any change. In such a case, the therapist may explore with the client the advantages and disadvantages of drinking and abstinence from alcohol and setting limits on drinking. Table 8.3 gives an example of this.

Finding alternative non-alcohol beverages (e.g. alcohol-free beers, non-alcoholic drinks), alternative activities to drinking in public

Date	Time	Where	Who with	Alcohol amount	Consequences
20/8	9 pm	Bert's Bar	John Robert	3 pints beer	Felt fine
21/8	6 pm	Bert's Bar	John Robert Malcolm Bobby	10 pints beer 1 whisky	Began to argue with Malcolm Bobby egged me on
	11 pm	Bobby's flat	Same people	5 cans beer	Wife nagged next day Row – hit her

Figure 8.1 Example of a drinking diary

places (e.g. playing football, cinema, playing pool, attending AA), setting limits on when and where alcohol might be consumed (e.g. only with certain individuals, after 9 p.m.) help to maintain the chosen drinking goal, whether that be a goal of abstinence or reduced consumption.

Anger problems

A problem often associated with those with Antisocial personality disorder is aggression. Difficulty in tolerating feelings of frustration and anger are common amongst this group of clients. In addition, many may have difficulty expressing anger appropriately.

The function of anger is often misunderstood. Like other emotions anger can help direct attention to a significant event in the environment. It also signals to other people displeasure and it can be used to influence and direct the behaviour of others. However, the way in

Table 8.3   Example: advantages and disadvantages of drinking and abstinence

Advantages of drinking	Disadvantages of drinking
1 Can go to pub with friends	1 Drink too much
2 Like the taste	2 Spend too much money
3 Helps me relax	3 Get hangovers
4 Alcohol makes me feel good	4 Makes me more likely to have rows with wife
	5 Get into serious trouble with the law
	6 Have to buy drinks for people I don't like

Advantages of abstinence	Disadvantages of abstinence
1 Won't get into trouble	1 Have to find other things to do
2 More money	2 I'd miss alcohol
3 Feel healthier	3 I don't think I could stick to no alcohol
4 More able to think straight	

which feelings of anger are acted upon is often inappropriate. It is often necessary to explain to clients that it is normal to feel angry but not always appropriate to behave aggressively. In general, clients who have problems with aggressive behaviour have difficulty understanding this distinction. The therapist can help to explain the distinction between feeling angry and acting aggressively by asking questions which help the client to analyse the situation which has engendered feelings of anger and an aggressive response.

Through questioning, the therapist can elicit the relationship between feeling angry and behaving aggressively and can help the client to become aware of how they can make an effective response as opposed to a response which will lead to further trouble. Joe had been in frequent fights with other men and reported intense feelings of rage and anger, even when the situation was apparently only mildly provoking. Below is an extract from a treatment session in which the therapist is asking Joe about an incident in a bar.

> ### Example: Analysis of situation in which Joe felt angry
>
> Situation: Joe went to a bar on his own but knew many people in the bar. The bar was very crowded and people were jostling each other to get a space at the bar. Just after Joe paid for his drink, a man pushed him and his drink spilled.
>
> *Th*: What did you want to do? (*emphasizes doing*)
> *J*: I wanted to smash his face in.

Th: How angry did you feel? (*states feeling*)

J: (*pause*) I was very angry. He just tried to walk away. In fact that's just what he did and I really lost my head. I shouted at him and some of the other men told me to calm down.

Th: What did you want to happen? (*goals*)

J: I'd have liked him to apologize and buy me another pint but he left.

Th: What stopped him buying you another drink then? (*seeks alternative explanation*)

J: Because he is an idiot.

Th: Any other reason? (*seeks alternative explanation*)

J: Because he's a coward and ran off.

Th: Was that because you were shouting at him?

J: I suppose so.

Th: The pub was busy – did he notice as he knocked your drink over?

J: No – he did not even notice – see how stupid he is?

Th: That doesn't sound like stupidity to me. It sounds like he just did not realize he had knocked over your pint. Is that possible? (*gives alternative explanation*)

J: I suppose so.

Th: So if someone does something and they don't notice what has happened, could it be just a mistake or an accident?

J: Yes it could have been an accident.

Th: So you would have smashed his face without thinking this through first eh? How would that have made you look? (*asks for consequences of behaviour*)

J: Stupid!

Th: So let's say you had evidence that he had noticed what he had done. He was aware that he had knocked over your pint and just turned away. You feel angry and you respond by wanting to smash his face. What would that achieve? (*consequences of original action*)

J: He would be on the floor – out cold.

Th: And he would not be able to either apologize or buy you another pint – is that right? (*achieve goal?*)

J: Yeah.

Th: So in one quick moment you have really lost out. He does not get the opportunity to say sorry and you don't get your pint of beer.

J: Yeah, I see your point.

Th: Could you have used your angry feelings to help you instead of hinder you from achieving your aim? After all, it was your pint he knocked over.

J: You mean I could have said something to him?

Th: Such as ...? Remember you are angry but this time you want to get what you want. (*seeks alternative way of solving problem*)

J: I could have said 'Hey pal – you knocked over my pint. How about buying me another one?'

Th: Well that certainly sounds direct and straight to the point and it gives you a good chance at getting what you want from the situation.

For Joe, the aim in this questioning was to teach him that he could have achieved what he wanted if he had perceived the other man's behaviour differently and not 'lost his head'. To do this, he would have had to take into account factors which were not immediately obvious to him, such as the bar being busy and the man bumping into him being accidental and not deliberate. One of Joe's core beliefs was that he had to be on his guard against other people as they would exploit him. This situation in the bar would have triggered Joe's belief as he would have perceived what happened as being non-accidental – in this case, other people would think that they could get off with knocking over his beer and not replacing it. So, rather than getting what he wanted, he got angry and the other man left. Helping Joe to be aware that there may be many factors influencing other people's behaviour and that his aggressive responses were unlikely to be as effective as an assertive response in achieving his goals was a key aspect of therapy.

As aggressive behaviour is likely to have resulted in problems, listing these subsequent problems is useful (see Table 8.4). Many clients find that the list of consequences can be long. Listing the pros and cons of using aggression can then be explored.

Social skills training and assertiveness training

Many clients will have few behavioural or cognitive skills to deal with anger. Social skills training and assertiveness training is often a highly appropriate part of treatment. Helping clients to develop body language and verbal skills which decrease the likelihood of an

Table 8.4 Example: pros and cons of behaving aggressively

Advantages	Disadvantages
Get my own way	The fights get worse
It gets people off my back	I'm getting older and can't fight so hard
It deals with problems quickly	the problems don't go away
	It costs me money in fines
	I may end up in deeper trouble

angry interpersonal situation escalating is essential, including how to remove oneself from a scene without loss of face.

Some clients will have difficulty expressing themselves appropriately with partners. Anger and aggression is often directed at partners. Interviewing a partner is essential for a full picture of the nature of the relationship, including its strengths and weaknesses.

For example, if the client reported aggressive episodes the therapist might carry out a detailed functional analysis, including antecedent factors such as the history of relationship problems, situational factors, pre-existing but related factors such as previous arguments, difficulties in modulating physiological arousal and current alcohol and drug consumption. The behaviour should be described in detail (e.g. was physical aggression used, were weapons used and towards whom). The consequences of the behaviour would include what happened immediately after an incident and what the likely pay-off (reinforcers) might be for having acted aggressively. Both long- and short-term consequences should be considered. It is only by carrying out such an individualized analysis can the therapist begin to understand the specific individual and situational factors which are involved and the functional significance of the behaviour itself.

Behavioural contracts

Behavioural contracts between couples may be helpful in moderating aggressive behaviours. The therapist can work on increasing problem-solving skills and assertiveness skills in both partners to reduce aggressive outbursts. Both partners need to be clear about the goals in reducing aggressive behaviour and the potential problems involved in attempting to make such changes. New, more adaptive behaviours need to replace more destructive behaviours. Agreeing and implementing such a contract between partners requires skills in negotiation on the part of the therapist. The therapist should avoid taking sides and should remain non-partisan. New behaviours need to be rehearsed frequently and the aim of developing these new, more adaptive ways of resolving conflict have to be re-stated over many sessions with both partners. If both partners can see an advantage in changing behaviour then they are more likely to work on the problems jointly and effectively.

Behavioural contracts with the therapist are also helpful in decreasing behaviours which impede progress in therapy. Contracts can be used to change specific behaviours such as non-attendance and verbal aggression within sessions. A 42-year-old man, Bill, with a diagnosis of Antisocial personality disorder initially did not attend therapy sessions on a regular basis. This interfered with treatment as little consistent progress could be made with therapy. After checking with Bill that he did want help with his problems, the therapist asked Bill to make a contract with her about attendance at sessions. She would continue to see him, over a number of sessions, providing that he attend every session or give appropriate notice of cancellation. If he failed to attend on two occasions without notice, she would discharge him. Had Bill not wanted help with his problems, she would have discharged him. This worked well and allowed the therapist to then work on the other main problem impeding progress in therapy, namely verbal aggression. Bill would shout at the therapist if she did not agree with him. He would also shout loudly when describing an event that had angered him in the period between treatment sessions. Staff in the adjacent clinical rooms had also complained to the therapist about Bill's loud swearing as it disturbed other clients. In order to continue seeing Bill in that clinical setting, he would have to modify his level of verbal aggression. Once Bill had clearly begun to attend regularly, the therapist chose a time when Bill was not too emotionally aroused to discuss his loud swearing. She asked him if he was aware of shouting loudly at times when he was 'stirred up' and if he knew how this affected others. Bill was aware of shouting and swearing and said that he thought others would know to not interfere with him when he was like this. The therapist agreed with Bill that others would probably stay away. She then told Bill that other therapists in the clinic had told her that their clients had complained about overhearing him shouting and swearing. This statement produced an immediate shift in Bill's perspective on this matter as he believed that he was 'talking in private' to the therapist and had clearly not considered the possibility that he could be overheard by strangers. He did not want others to hear him discussing his problems with his therapist. The therapist then discussed other possible disadvantages which Bill's behaviour may have had in the past. After some discussion Bill agreed that he did not want others to hear his business and he agreed with the therapist not to raise his voice beyond a level that was acceptable to her or which could be heard through the clinic wall by others. They agreed that during treatment she would raise her hand as a signal to him that his voice was too loud and that he would abide by her signal.

Poor literacy skills

Difficulties in reading and writing may be evident in this group of clients. This may be due to childhood problems that resulted in being unable to benefit from schooling. Often clients with Antisocial personality disorder report having attended school irregularly or having been uninterested in school work. Being unable to fully comprehend written language can be a source of frustration and confusion and can lead to a sense of alienation. Sensitivity is needed when asking about reading and writing ability as most people hide such difficulties from others. During initial sessions with a client, the therapist will have an opportunity to cover the client's school experience and attendance and this can provide an opportunity to ask about reading and writing skills. As many clients are ashamed of having such difficulties, it is often helpful to point out that these are relatively common problems and that most people have some problems in this area. Clients who have such problems can be encouraged to attend adult literacy classes.

For clients with such difficulties, any written materials will need to be adapted appropriately. Using diagrams to explain a formulation, using highly structured forms and adapting homework records and clinic handouts are all essential to overcome poor literacy skills. Clients themselves will have developed ways of coping with written communications and these methods can be exploited by the therapist.

Constructive activity

A poor work record may be common to clients with personality disorders. The therapist should attempt to consider the factors involved in a history of employment and attempt to differentiate where such problems are due to the individual's attitude towards work and work behaviour or to more local economic factors such as availability of suitable and appropriate work. Graded tasks can be utilized to improve such problems as work attendance and concentration at work. For those who are unemployed, and who are seeking employment, scheduling work finding can be helpful. Setting aside specific times in the week to visit job centres or read the jobs vacant columns in newspapers as well as telephoning for information and completing applications are some examples. In the absence of availability of work, or when the client appears unwilling to consider employment, the client and therapist have to consider finding alternative satisfying activities to structure daily life. Constructive use of one's time is a clear expectation of therapy as this is assumed to improve both quality and satisfaction of life.

Typical behavioural problems: Borderline personality disorder

The previous chapter outlined some of the more typical problems of individuals with Antisocial personality disorder. This chapter concentrates on the behavioural problems that are common to individuals with Borderline personality disorder. Clients with Borderline personality disorder suffer from a wide array of problems and their clinical presentation can vary. None the less, behavioural techniques can be used throughout treatment in conjunction with cognitive techniques. Again, a detailed formulation and an analysis of problem behaviours is an essential first step in treatment. Sometimes this task is made more difficult because Borderline clients often lack analytical skills and tend to describe problems and situations in a global, undifferentiated style. The therapist may often have to spend a considerable amount of time in training a client to analyse a situation or problem behaviourally. The effort involved is well spent as this skill is essential to effective treatment.

Treatment focus

Although the problems of Borderline patients may vary, they can however be characterized as being within the affective, cognitive, interpersonal and behavioural domains. Although the cognitive model places central importance on an individual's beliefs and assumptions, these are regarded as 'influencing the perception and interpretation of events and in shaping both behavioural and emotional responses' (Beck *et al.*, 1990: 186). As Borderline clients

Table 9.1 Examples of problems and treatment strategies in borderline clients

Problem	Treatment strategy
Suicidal ideation or attempt	Therapist management Risk assessment Assessment of depression Problem list Reasons for living Self-care and making the environment safer
Deliberate self harm	Functional analysis Motive for behaviour Understanding the emotion Alternative adaptive behaviours Self-care
Mood disturbance	Distraction Meditation Opposite mood induction Knowing it will pass

see themselves as unacceptable, powerless and vulnerable, and the world and others as malevolent, they are likely to behave in ways that directly relate to these themes. For example, clients often wish to harm themselves and have a tendency to form unstable relationships with others. Not infrequently, Borderline clients have a tendency to have periods of relative stability followed by crises when feelings of powerlessness and unacceptability predominate. As a result, they have difficulty being consistent in terms of desired life goals. In addition, individuals suffering from Borderline personality disorder may present to health professionals with a wide variety of psychiatric disorders such as depression, anxiety, psychosomatic disorders, eating disorders and with problems resulting from childhood sexual abuse. These disorders and problems need to be treated along with the problems relating to personality disorder.

Borderline clients require a variety of different treatment strategies and again, case formulation is the key to establishing an overall understanding of the problems and which problems should be given priority in treatment. Problems such as suicidal behaviour and deliberate self-harm are given the highest priority in treatment. Table 9.1 gives some examples of the types of problems that clinicians may encounter in treating Borderline clients and the treatment strategies that may be helpful in their management.

Order of treatment tasks

Behaviours which cause harm to self are given the highest priority in treatment. If behaviours such as overdoses and self-mutilation are not tackled in a systematic way early in therapy, treatment will tend to be crisis-driven. If ignored, these behaviours will not dissipate and will produce a chaos factor into treatment which is unhelpful and wasteful of treatment time.

Assessing suicidal risk

The therapist should be alert to the presence of the risk of suicidal behaviour. This involves paying attention to thoughts of suicide as well as to suicidal behaviours. The therapist has to make an assessment of the degree of risk of a client completing a suicidal act and should consider hospitalization as an option. This can be both an appropriate response and beneficial to the client if there is an immediate requirement for the client to be in a safe environment as the act of removing an individual from the immediate environment can help to let a crisis period pass.

The therapist should attempt to assess the strength of the client's intention to commit suicide. Asking about symptoms of depression, levels of hopelessness or specific plans to commit suicide will help the therapist to assess the risk involved. Questions relating to the method considered, the availability of support from others and whether or not the client has told anyone else, are factors which might also be taken into account in assessing risk. If in any doubt, the therapist should seek a medical opinion or the opinion of a supervisor in assessing the risk of suicide and in assessing whether the client might benefit from hospitalization.

Suicidal ideation or attempt

The therapist has to make an assessment of the client's reasons for considering suicide or making a suicide attempt. The assumption in cognitive therapy for Borderline clients is the same as in cognitive therapy for depressed clients: individual clients have their own motives for considering suicide and have come to the conclusion that this may be a desirable option (Blackburn and Davidson, 1990). Conveying to the client that the problem is being taken seriously and being empathic and understanding of the client's distress can help to relieve a client's sense of isolation and distress. The therapist's goal is then to redress the balance in favour of living rather than dying. The therapist has to do this in a very direct manner, often providing evidence for the client that the balance is in favour of living. In order to accomplish this, the therapist has to use evidence from the client, the client's personal history and how the client has overcome difficulties in the past. It can also be useful to provide accounts of other clients' difficulties and how these were overcome. It is assumed that the client's view of their problems has become extremely narrow and that the client has lost sight of other potential ways of resolving problems.

Hopelessness, depression, overwhelming social, financial and personal problems, or trying to influence or even get back at others are common motives given for considering suicide. Negative automatic thoughts associated with hopelessness can be elicited and modified using standard cognitive techniques. By establishing a problem list with the client, the therapist can break down the client's sense of feeling overwhelmed. The therapist has to remain problem-oriented yet empathic to the client's level of distress. As the client is likely to have a negative view of self, world and future, cognitive techniques can be used to modify dysfunctional thoughts and perceptions.

Reasons for living

The therapist can also help the client to draw up a list of advantages and disadvantages for living and dying (see Table 9.2). It is always very important to be specific about reasons for living as many clients who wish to die have only vague reasons for living and find providing highly specific reasons to remain alive a difficult task. By listing the advantages and disadvantages for dying, the therapist pays attention to the client's reasons for dying as well as tipping the balance in favour of living. It is useful to give a copy of the work done in the session to the client to take home. This will provide a source of evidence which may mitigate against future feelings of hopelessness as a client may continue to be vulnerable when alone.

Many clients also benefit greatly from discussing ways in which they can keep themselves safe from self-harm and this can help to decrease their sense of hopelessness and being out of control. Coming to some agreement with the therapist about what plans or safety strategies will be implemented is necessary before arranging another appointment. For many clients, this involves making their home environments safer by throwing away unused medications, razor blades and alcohol, which make self-harm more likely.

Some clients will resist getting rid of all excess medication or cutting instruments at first, claiming that they wish to have the option of harming themselves should things get really awful for

Table 9.2 Example: advantages and disadvantages of living and dying

Advantages of dying	*Advantages of living*
1 I won't feel anything	1 I am getting help to solve my problems
2 I will get rid of my problems	2 I will see C's children grow up. The children like me and I am important to them
	3 I can ask John and Carol for help in getting work. They can help me to write application forms
	4 Carol and John have told me that I can stay at their house if I feel down and lonely
	5 My mother would be very distressed if I killed myself. She would always feel that I did not ask her for help. Although we have a difficult relationship, I have never really spent time talking to her about her life and how she feels and how she has managed to cope without my father

Disadvantages of dying	*Disadvantages of living*
1 Carol and John would feel terrible	1 I will have to put up with the way I am
2 I won't ever know if my life could have been better	
3 There would be no going back	

them. Therapists should explore this motivation further. Ask the client if having these substances or instruments present makes them think less or more about harming themselves. Does it remind them of their previous episodes of self-harm and does this make them feel better or worse about themselves? What would they say to someone who had a dependence on alcohol who kept a bottle of alcohol in the wardrobe?

After the disadvantages of keeping such substances or instruments has been explored, it is important to re-attribute the client's desire to self-harm as the sole option. For all clients, an episode of wanting to self-harm is an important signal to seek help and to protect themselves, not to harm themselves.

Another strategy recommended by Thomas Ellis and Cory Newman (1996) involves encouraging the client to delay suicidal impulses by reflecting on all the things they have been meaning to get round to doing in their lives but have, for some reason, put off. They suggest getting the client to generate a list of things and why they might be important to the client. One client, Sarah, wrote that she wanted to visit the Scottish Highlands as she had never had the opportunity and had always felt better when surrounded by Nature's beauty. She also wrote that she wanted to learn how to paint as a way of expressing herself; also that she wanted to take her nieces out to the theatre but had never been able to afford to do this, but could save a little money every week and take them to see a pantomime as a Christmas present. These plans helped Sarah to buy into life again and to become less hopeless about her future.

Some clients can repeatedly use parasuicidal behaviour or threats of suicide to gain attention and help from others. The therapist has to attempt to understand the function of such behaviour for the client and the consequences of such behaviour. For some clients, repeated overdoses are a means of generating crisis situations, which in turn are attempts at eliciting helping and caring behaviour from others. The client's behaviour is inadvertently reinforced by the attention received, which in turn increases the chances of such behaviour being repeated. This is seldom an effective strategy for the client. Those who may have responded in a caring and supportive manner to the client in the past, often find that their efforts to help appear to be insufficient or rejected when the client attempts self-harm again. 'Carers' and 'helpers' then become frustrated in their attempts to help and may withdraw support from the client. Clients who repeatedly self-harm are often very angry and irritable and their unstable moods make it difficult for others to remain sympathetic. In order to decrease the frequency of such self-harming behaviour, the therapist has to attempt to change the contingencies operating in such a way as to reinforce more adaptive ways of signalling distress whilst reducing self-destructive behaviours.

The therapist does this by taking the client very seriously. The therapist acknowledges that the client's life is difficult and that problems may seem to be overwhelming. By taking the client's attempts at serious self-harm or suicidal threats very seriously, the therapist acknowledges the client's distress. The therapist however points out to the client that there may be other ways of resolving problems rather than suicidal behaviour. As in dialectical behaviour therapy (Linehan, 1993a), the therapist has to take a non-negotiable position on reducing deliberate self-harm as this behaviour does not improve the client's quality of life and may lead to an increased likelihood of subsequent suicide.

One problem which can arise is the client's attempts at drawing the therapist into a parasuicidal crisis. If a client telephones a therapist having taken an overdose, the therapist has to make an assessment of the medical seriousness of the overdose. If a client reports having taken an overdose, and it is not possible to judge the potential seriousness of this action, then the client's medical doctor has to be informed. If the client has not taken a serious overdose, and the therapist is confident of this fact, the therapist should encourage the client that it is their responsibility to seek appropriate medical help, if necessary. The client has to be managed sympathetically but firmly. The therapist should then ask the client to attend at the next available appointment to discuss the incident and the problems he or she is experiencing.

Self-caring

Many clients, including those with Borderline personality disorder, have difficulty in caring for themselves. They often try desperately to elicit protective and nurturing behaviour from others but appear to be unable to protect and nurture themselves. Clients will readily recognize that this is the case but still have little idea about how to go about caring for themselves. The therapist's task is to aid the client in developing behaviours that are self-nurturing. Borderline clients frequently recognize that they are able to be nurturing to others. The therapist has to explicitly instruct clients to protect and nurture themselves. For some clients, this can be insisting that the client eats regular meals and gets enough rest and sleep. For others the task is more complicated, as they appear to act impulsively and in a chaotic manner. Learning to slow down, think before acting and to behave in a protective manner towards themselves is helpful. One client, Susan, developed a 'stop and protect myself' motto for times when she began to feel out of control. She had several strategies to help her at these times but the two most favoured options were to phone or visit a person whom she trusted to be fair minded and whose opinion she valued or alternatively doing something soothing such as stroking and cuddling her cat.

Another client, who was finding her lack of employment and home life intolerable, decided that the best way in which she could be kind to herself would be to have some 'time out'. She would go to bed and ask her family to leave her alone for a few hours. During this time, she cosseted herself and tried not to attempt to resolve any problems. She arranged the bed so that it would be comfortable and she had some of her favourite books and music tapes around her if she wished to be distracted from her problems although the main aim was to rest quietly and be caring to herself. This client described her strategy as helping to build a floor underneath her which she would not fall through. One of the main advantages of her strategy was that she was not, at these times, faced with her own expectations that she should solve her problems and so, run the risk of experiencing the intense sense of failing to resolve anything. In addition, giving her permission to be caring of herself and non-judgemental brought about a shift in her basic assumption that she was to blame for everything that went wrong and should be punished or humiliated.

The sky is not the limit

Most clients with this disorder appear to take on too much when they begin to feel better about themselves, have experienced more stable mood and have reduced self-harm. It is as if the non-coping self is switched off and they have to rapidly move into a coping mode where they expect themselves to be able to take on new challenges and immediately resume previous commitments. At these times, the client is particularly vulnerable to relapse.

Naïve therapists may welcome this stoical aspect of clients but it is often more appropriate to explore the client's core beliefs and assumptions at these times. One client, whose core belief was 'I am useless', described how at times of greater stability, she would 'flip' to a belief that she *should* cope with everything. She also thought that if she did not cope at these times, it would prove that she was useless. This suggested that her core belief about being useless was still dominant but operating in a dichotomous, all or nothing, manner. The important lesson for this client was to learn not to try to do too much at these times. Instead she was encouraged to carry out behavioural experiments where she tested out how much she could do without feeling overwhelmed and unable to cope. This incremental approach allowed her to build up her capacity to cope with more active days and more interaction with others without feeling stretched to capacity. She called this process learning not to reach for the sky.

Deliberate self-harm

Individuals with Borderline personality disorder often deliberately harm themselves. This behaviour is not necessarily the same as harming oneself with the aim of ending one's life. Cutting arms and legs with razor blades, severely scratching wrists and forearms with sharp instruments, stabbing at stomachs and breasts are some examples of this type of self-harm. Very often such self-harm is carried out in private but Borderline clients will often display scars to the therapist and expect these to be noticed. Usually this type of self-harm occurs in response to dysphoric mood states. Clients will

Table 9.3 Example: functional analysis of self-harm behaviours

What happened before self-harm?	2 hours before: meal with parents. They were not talking to each other. I felt stuck in the middle, couldn't eat
Feelings leading up to self-destructive act	Numbness
Associated thoughts	I feel nothing. I am nothing
Self-destructive behaviour	Scratched thighs with razor blade
Feelings	No one feeling; pain on cutting
Associated thoughts	At least I feel pain; I can feel something
Consequences	More marks on thighs Blood on clothes Feel ashamed Hate self Have to avoid swimming Problems still there Cannot avoid them
Alternative to slashing	Go to bed and sleep or listen to loud music Tense my muscles really hard Melt ice cubes in my hand

sometimes say that they feel 'nothing' before cutting and the action of cutting results in some sense of relief from this mood state which is difficult to tolerate. The antecedents of this behaviour often need careful assessment. Although the behaviour may be in response to dysphoric mood, there is often a triggering event that the client has been unable to cope with effectively. For some, however, no apparent antecedent event can be found and it appears that the self-harm behaviour is in response to mood state alone. The aim of therapy is to reduce such behaviours and help the client to deal more effectively with dysphoric mood states. Table 9.3 gives an example of a functional analysis of self-harm behaviour.

Mood disturbance

Clients who repeatedly self-harm often feel intensely angry with themselves and with others but feel ashamed of these feelings and find it hard to discuss this with their therapists. Such emotions can become overwhelming as the client struggles to either avoid or control strong emotions. Often clients, particularly clients with Borderline personality disorders, have experienced others as ignoring or invalidating their emotions in childhood. An example of this might be being told as a child that you should not cry or be upset because you are cold, hungry and tired and cannot go to bed when in fact it would be reasonable and understandable to be upset and want to sleep. Another example is being told that you should feel happy about something when in fact you only feel relieved. Marsha Linehan (1993a) has described the conflict that such clients experience as they struggle to invalidate and suppress their own emotional experience. Having learnt through experience that expressing intense negative emotions is punished, the client fails to trust their own emotional responses, is unable to articulate and express emotions verbally and behaviourally, and becomes confused about their own perception of experience.

Many clients have difficulty tolerating dysfunctional mood states. The therapist has to be alert to the client developing a depressive disorder. For most clients, however, the main difficulty will be in dealing with distressed emotional states that may last up to several days at a time; most mood states, however, tend to be more transitory, although no less intense and distressing. Using cognitive techniques will be helpful here but increasing the client's tolerance of these negative mood states is also important. In order to do this, the client has to be willing to experience the dysphoric mood state and not suppress it.

Tolerating dysfunctional mood states

Jon Kabat-Zinn and others (1992) have suggested that meditation or mindfulness techniques can be helpful in learning to tolerate dysfunctional mood states. Essentially, the client is trained to concentrate by focusing on a restricted field. For example, one could focus on breathing, or the way one's body feels sitting on a chair. By this focusing of attention, a client can become aware of thoughts and feelings but is now able to observe these in a dispassionate way. Essentially the client learns to 'stand back' from the distressing feelings and thoughts and to become a participating observer. Thoughts and feelings are simply accepted and experienced as 'objects' rather than as imperatives to action. This has the effect of emotions being accepted for what they are and not reacted on. Clients need to practise this frequently in order to gain a sense of mastery. To their surprise, many clients find this very helpful.

Linehan (1993a) has developed core mindfulness skills as part of dialectical behaviour therapy (DBT) for Borderline clients. These skills involve rather similar techniques. DBT teaches clients to attend to events that may be distressing and to experience whatever is happening rather than trying to stop the emotion. The idea here is based on exposure as a method of extinguishing automatic responses of avoidance and fear. Mindfulness is described as participating with attention (Linehan, 1993a). Clients are also encouraged to take a non-judgmental stance and to do what is 'effective' as opposed to what may seem to them to be 'the right thing to do'.

Other techniques involve doing the opposite of mindfulness: using distraction and finding activities which will allow the client to concentrate on the task in hand to the exclusion of the negative mood state. The idea here is that by deliberately taking attention away from feelings such as guilt, hopelessness and low mood the client can gain some reprieve from the mood state. These activities have to be absorbing and may often involve physical effort. Examples are scrubbing the kitchen floor, doing aerobic exercises, taking a brisk walk, having a cold shower and reading aloud.

Inducing incompatible mood states

Another technique for tolerating dysfunctional mood states involves deliberately inducing mood states which are incompatible with or opposite to the negative mood state (Linehan, 1993b). Playing pleasant, soothing or up-beat music, watching a funny or spellbinding film, meeting a friend who is more positive about life, moving face muscles into a smile or doing something to help someone else are all possibilities.

Reminding the client that the mood state will pass

Some clients find the knowledge that negative mood states can pass helpful. The therapist seeks evidence from the client about how they have coped in the past with negative mood states. Keeping to hand a written record of the evidence that distressing mood states are temporary can be useful. For example, one client kept a card with this information at her bedside and in her handbag as a reminder.

It can also be helpful to place some intrinsic value on having suffered, telling the client that those who have suffered are often better and more understanding of other people's problems as they have personal experience which has deepened and widened their understanding of both negative and positive aspects of life (Linehan, 1993a).

The motivation for self-mutilation and other self-destructive behaviours need to be understood by the therapist. Again, a detailed functional analysis of the antecedents, behaviour and consequences needs to be obtained. The associated thoughts and feelings need to be explored by the therapist. After the therapist has understood the motivation for self-mutilation, more functionally adaptive behaviours can be gradually substituted for the self-destructive behaviours.

Childhood sexual abuse

Some researchers have found a link between Borderline personality disorder and childhood sexual abuse (e.g. Brown and Anderson, 1991). This will not apply to all clients with this disorder but therapists need to be aware that at least some of their clients will have suffered from sexual abuse as children. Although some clients will divulge that they have been sexually abused in childhood at assessment or during treatment, others will remain silent on the subject, perhaps feeling unsure about whether or not to trust the therapist with such a disclosure. The therapist must therefore take the initiative in broaching the subject with clients.

The following are thought to be some indicators of sexual abuse:

• women with a history of repeated victimization
• alcohol- or drug-dependent women
• women whose mothers were ill or absent from home
• women who had taken adult care-taking responsibilities for home and family from early age.

These indicators can be kept in mind when seeing any client. A straightforward question such as ' Have you at any time been touched by someone in a sexual manner when you did not want to be?' allows the client the opportunity to tell the therapist if any form of sexual abuse has ever occurred. Some clients may not feel able to bring up the topic, even when asked directly, and so the therapist may give the client other opportunities to do so if they think this is indicated.

The list below indicates possible ways of helping clients to feel comfortable about disclosing childhood sexual abuse:

• Ask directly if sexual abuse occurred during childhood.
• Use a structured questionnaire to obtain complete sexual history.
• Define incest for the client.
• Ask about best and worst experiences of childhood.

If a client does disclose that they have been sexually abused in childhood, or for that matter, in adulthood, the reaction of the therapist is important in determining what happens next. Both men and women who have been sexually abused are frequently hypersensitive to the attitude of other people towards them. They may feel disgusted and ashamed of themselves and any slightly negative expression or act on the therapist's part can reinforce the client's attitude towards themselves and may confirm that they should not have told anyone. It is also important that the therapist does not express a quick opinion about the abuser as the client may have positive as well as negative feelings towards the abuser. Understanding how the client views the sexual abuse and the exact nature of their relationship with the abuser needs to be clarified. This does not mean that the therapist should condone the abuse, but rather seek to find out the facts of the case and whether or not the abuse continues.

After a client has told the therapist that they have been sexually abused, it is important that the therapist does not then ignore what the client has said. A calm, empathic stance and encouragement and praise for having disclosed such a difficult experience helps the client to feel a sense of trust in the therapist and a sense of relief for having told someone about the abuse. The therapist should never minimize the importance of the disclosure.

The treatment of problems which may arise from childhood sexual abuse can be dealt with in a cognitive therapy framework. The psychological meaning of the abuse should be the focus of treatment rather than specific details of the abuse, although some clients do find it helpful to go through specific incidents of abuse with the therapist. In general, the client's view of themselves and others is likely to be the focus of therapy. Issues of trust, autonomy, responsibility and sexuality are likely to be raised by the client.

There are many useful texts published on the assessment and therapy of adults who have been sexually abused as children. For female clients, the work of Burke Draucher (1992) and Hall and Lloyd (1993) is particularly recommended, and for male clients who have survived sexual abuse, that of Mendel (1995).

Clinical evaluation of change

As cognitive therapy aims to change specific and agreed targets, therapists and clients are able to evaluate changes in these targets with treatment. With clients with personality disorders, the degree of change may not be as dramatic or as quick when compared to those who do not have personality disorders and the therapist has to be realistic in their expectations about what can be achieved. None the less, important and clinically significant changes can be achieved with some, if not all clients with personality disorders with treatment. As many of the client's problems are long-standing, changes in cognition, emotion and behaviour may happen slowly and will need to be maintained to have any lasting effect. Regular evaluation of the effectiveness of therapy is essential if the therapist and client are to know if therapy is succeeding and should be continued, or if the approach is not helpful and should be discontinued.

Outcome of therapy

Evaluating the outcome of therapy for an individual client begins at the start of therapy when the target problems have been defined and agreed. For each client there will be a unique set of problems and agreed targets of treatment can be measured and changes assessed.

Measuring change in target problems

The therapist has to know to what extent or magnitude the problem affected the client before coming to therapy. For some problems, the client can provide a clear retrospective account of the extent of these. For example, clients can often provide information on the number of overdoses or self-harm episodes within a limited time frame. For other problems, baseline data may need to be gathered before a clear description of the frequency or degree of the problem can be assessed. Any changes in the target problem with therapy can then be evaluated against baseline or retrospective accounts of the problem.

Some target problems are relatively easily defined and measured whereas others require to be re-stated in order to measure change. Some problems, such as a difficulty tolerating unpleasant mood states, are more difficult to define and measure. This type of problem is common in clients with Borderline personality disorder and similar problems, such as feeling angry, are common in clients with Antisocial personality disorder.

The following example illustrates how this type of problem might be monitored during treatment.

Example: the assessment of feelings of anger

Stage 1: Therapist and client define the target problem

An agreed definition is reached with the client of feelings of anger which arise in response to some event or at other times when thinking about past events. This is best phrased in the client's own words such as 'I feel keyed up and sometimes my heart starts to race.' 'I often feel like I want to smash someone or something.' 'Occasionally I smash something.' 'At the worst, I have hit someone.'

Stage 2: Measurement to be used

Scale of 0 to 5: Feeling angry

0 No feelings of anger
1 Slight feeling of being a bit annoyed or angry. No desire to smash something or someone. Can easily distract myself from this feeling
2 Recognize I feel angry but still able to control these feelings and to stop thinking about it but needs more effort than in (1). No desire to smash something or someone
3 Moderate degree of feeling angry but still in control of desire to smash something or someone. Difficulty in stopping thinking about whatever has made me angry
4 Feeling very angry. Want to smash something or

someone but do not. Cannot stop thinking about whatever has made me angry and getting really worked up
5 Intense feeling of anger. Smash something or someone

Stage 3: Agree on the frequency of measurement

From preliminary information about the frequency of
feeling angry, it was agreed that recordings would be
taken in the morning, afternoon and during the evening
and any precipitating event noted so that discussion of the
events could take place in sessions.

Stage 4: Method of measuring

This client monitored his feelings of anger in a weekly diary
(see Figure 10.1) and the example shows that enough
information was collated to help discussion in sessions.
Asking this client to record incidents in more detail would
have been counterproductive as he was not practised in
recording information.

Stage 5: Assess progress regularly

As therapy is arranged in blocks of treatment and an overall
assessment of progress is reviewed at these points, the
therapist can collate and summarize the client's data on
target problems at this point to gain an overview of
progress.

The weekly records were summarized in chart form to
assess progress in treatment over 10 sessions. The total
weekly anger scores were then recorded on a chart. This
chart (Figure 10.2) showed an overall reduction in the
degree to which he felt angry over the 10 weeks of
treatment. Although not shown here, this client's baseline
data indicated that he was scoring in the range between 25
and 35 in the weeks before his problem with feeling angry
became a treatment target.

This chart allowed both the therapist and client to see at
a glance that he had felt less angry over the 10 sessions.
Daily ratings of degree of anger could have been presented
to the client but as these would have shown quite large
fluctuations, the therapist preferred to demonstrate change
to this client using a summary score of degree of anger
recorded over each week. Presenting data in a visual, as
opposed to a numerical, form is an effective method of
conveying a relatively large quantity of data to a client.

	Monday	Tuesday	Wednesday	Thursday	Friday	Saturday	Sunday
Morning	0	0	Letter from ex-wife demanding money 2	Phone for advice from lawyer 3	Went out fishing with friend 0	0	1
Afternoon	0	0	Phoned lawyer 3	3	1	1	0
Evening	0	1	Frustrated 4	Spoke to my friend 2	2	0	1
Late evening	0	1	Still frustrated 4	Calmed down 1	1	0	0

Figure 10.1 Weekly diary: rating of the degree to which you felt angry

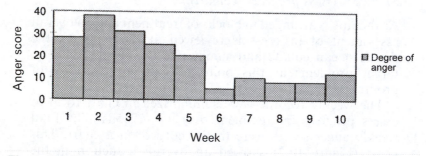

Figure 10.2 Degree of anger over 10 weeks recorded in chart form

Record of new, more effective ways of thinking and behaving

The information gathered as part of working on schema change is also a measure of progress in treatment. The client's notebook used throughout therapy contains valuable information on how the client has changed their thinking and behaviour and is a permanent record of progress in treatment. For example, change in core beliefs can be assessed regularly on a continuum and new behaviours that are indicative of such a change can be recorded.

As a client's overall social functioning is important in the treatment of personality disorder, a record of this can be kept throughout treatment. The following example illustrates how this might be done.

> ### Example: record of social functioning
>
> Jackie, a client with a diagnosis of Borderline personality disorder, stated at the beginning of treatment that she had few social contacts and had difficulty developing friend-ships. At the beginning of treatment, Jackie and the therapist kept a record of the names of people with whom she came in contact. After a few sessions, Jackie selected four women at work whom she thought were friendly and trustworthy and recorded her social contacts with them. As she had difficulty making friends, she was encouraged to take steps in getting to know these individuals. After the first 10 sessions of treatment, her record of contacts with these four women was evaluated in terms of the number of social contacts which had been pleasurable. This 'positive log' helped Jackie to be more aware of people who were friendly in her immediate social network. Deliberately recording these pleasurable social contacts helped Jackie to focus her attention on those whom she could trust and be more friendly towards rather than on her core belief that she was bad and that no-one would like her. Her new more adaptive belief was that she was 'okay' as a person and that other people might like her some of the time.
>
> Jackie's record of contacts with people who seemed to be friendly towards her is shown in Figure 10.3.
>
> #### Jackie's summary
>
> I have been able to talk to these four women regularly and although at first I was quite worried that they would not like me and that they might make fun of me, I have got to know them a little better and we seem to get on well. They have told me some things about themselves and I have begun to tell them some things about myself. Jenny has asked me over to her flat for the evening and I have taken the risk of asking Caroline to come with me to the canteen for lunch and she was positive about this. I'm still a bit apprehensive about making friends but now I notice when others are being friendly towards me.

Week	Jenny	Caroline	Wilma	Sarah	Total contacts
1	✓✓	–	–	✓	3
2	✓✓✓	✓	✓	✓	6
3	✓✓✓	✓	✓	✓	6
4	✓✓✓✓	✓✓	✓	✓	8
5	✓✓✓	✓✓✓	–	–	6
6	–	–	–	–	(Had flu)
7	✓✓✓✓	✓✓	✓	✓	8
8	✓✓✓	✓✓✓	✓✓	✓✓	10
9	✓✓✓✓✓	✓✓✓✓	✓✓	✓	12
10	✓✓✓	✓✓✓	✓	✓✓	9

Figure 10.3 Chart record showing the number of social contacts that were pleasurable

Asking significant others

In addition, if therapy has involved significant others, either in the assessment of problems or in therapy itself, their view of the client's interpersonal functioning is very useful in monitoring change and their assessment of progress with treatment is often pertinent and hopefully encouraging for the client. There are, of course, occasions when the therapist might judge that asking a significant other for feedback would not be appropriate. For example, it would not be wise to ask for feedback from a significant other who undermined a client or who was in a damaging relationship with the client and where part of the therapy had focused on how the client might change this relationship.

The therapist's ending summary of treatment

By the end of treatment the therapist may have written several summaries of sessions for the client and will have given the client a copy of the agreed formulation. These summaries to the client can be placed in a special folder for the client and presented as a record of treatment. Most client's appreciate this gesture and the record provides an *aide-mémoire* for the future. The following example is the therapist's final summary to Jackie.

Example: Therapist's final summary to Jackie

July 10th

To Jackie

We have now met on 18 occasions over a year to work together on your problems. When you first came to see me we talked a lot about the problems you had been experiencing and how these had arisen. We have tried to understand these difficulties. Your main problems at the beginning were that you were very isolated and had no friends and that you were cutting yourself. You described your mood as being seriously up and down and you did not know what you wanted to do with your life or indeed who you were. Many of these problems were long-standing and you felt very hopeless about your future.

In therapy you became aware that you believed that you were a bad person and that you thought others would not like you. You were very scared of being friendly and open with other people because you thought that they would reject you or make fun of you. You found it very hard to cope with your negative moods and when you felt overwhelmed you were often tempted to take an overdose. You cut yourself when you felt 'frozen' emotionally or when you had some memories of your childhood, particularly of when you were sexually abused by your stepfather.

Some of the first few years of your life were quite happy but you also remember your mother and father arguing and fighting and your mother crying a lot. Your parents divorced when you were 6 years old and you never saw much of your father after that . When he left, you thought that you must have been bad as he did not get in touch with you for many months. As a child it was easier for you to think that you had done something wrong rather than assume that the adults around you were uncaring. Through talking to your mother again, you are now aware that she did not want your father to see you as she wanted to punish him for leaving her for another woman. You, of course, did not know this as a child. Your mother became quite depressed after your father left and you think that she may have been drinking heavily at that time. This was a very confusing time for you as your mother stopped showing you affection and did not seem to notice that you were also very upset about losing your father. You thought that you were bad and that you should not be upset as this would upset your mother.

Your mother married again when you were 9 years old and from the beginning you did not like your step-father. He always wanted you to cuddle him and when he was drunk, he abused you. Again you thought you were bad as he told you not to tell anyone. Now you realize that he was wrong to do this and that you were *not* responsible. You were a little girl whom no one protected.

When you were 14 you tried to tell your mother about what your step-father was doing to you but she did not believe you and spoke up in his defence. This was very confusing for you and you thought that no one cared about you or believed you. What happened to you was awful and no one deserves to be treated like this. It seems that all of these experiences lead you to conclude that you were a bad person and as you had no one whom you could trust and talk to, this belief was never challenged. You left home after you took your first overdose. This was a courageous step for you to take as you had little experience of the world and you felt alone and no one seemed to care, except the social worker and your doctor.

In therapy, you have tried to develop new ways of thinking about yourself. You know that you are not bad – you now think and believe that you are a worthwhile and 'okay' person. You have kept a very clear record of examples of being 'okay' as a person. This has been difficult for you to do as before you really did not notice things which would have suggested you were 'okay'. The old belief that you were bad seemed to dominate the way you perceived everything. Your new belief is strengthening and I'm glad that you can now recognize that you have intrinsic worth as a person as well as many examples of new ways of thinking about yourself as 'okay'.

You have also been developing new strategies to look after yourself. You are making friendships with some women and they have welcomed you into their lives. You have started to eat better food, take more breaks from work, and to keep yourself safe when you feel like harming yourself. I think you have done very well at making these changes and I know how you have struggled to keep up these changes.

We have concentrated on your future more recently. You have decided to do another course to give you better qualifications. You went and asked your manager to support you in this and he has agreed to fund you through the course. He told you that your work was valued and that you have shown yourself to be a diligent and capable colleague. You have also decided not to put off doing some things that you would like to do such as buying yourself a new music system and going walking with a rambler's group. This is part of your new desire to look after yourself and to be generous to yourself. You have always been generous to others, both in kind and in giving of your own time. Now it is time to be good to yourself too.

I wish you well in your future, Jackie.

With my best wishes

11

Ending treatment

The final stage

The final stage of therapy is as important as any other stage but it is often neglected by therapists. The significance of treatment ending, particularly in the treatment of those with personality disorder, is likely to depend on two factors: the therapeutic relationship and the client's specific beliefs about loss. For many clients, the end of therapy is already being discussed and explored at the beginning of treatment. Clients who are afraid of abandonment, or who have experienced loss in the past are likely to be particularly sensitive to the finite nature of therapy and for them, this may even have implications for engagement in therapy. Unless beliefs about loss and abandonment are addressed at the beginning of therapy, little progress will be made and the client may be reluctant to engage in any therapy, and may not disclose problems or will have difficulty building up a trusting relationship with the therapist. For these patients, the end of therapy begins at the beginning.

For some, therapy in itself can be a primary source of activity and the therapist may be one of the few human contacts the client experiences on a regular basis. It is important that the therapist addresses this explicitly and conveys clearly to the client that therapy is not an end in itself and that part of the client's responsibility in entering therapy is to improve social relationships or, in some cases, make the beginning of relationships with others. Many clients are extremely socially isolated and, with limited financial resources, have little opportunity to meet other people socially. Making social contacts or finding satisfying and purposeful structured activities involving others are often some of the main behavioural goals in treatment.

Negotiating the ending date

As the final stage of therapy approaches, it is helpful to have a clear ending date. As cognitive therapy is goal-directed and progress in therapy is regularly reviewed, the treatment will have clearly defined phases. An ending date should be negotiated with the client as the final stage of treatment is reached to signal that therapy is coming to an end. The therapist has the responsibility to discuss this with the client and, in collaboration, they can discuss what can realistically be achieved within the final stage of the current therapeutic contract. The length of the final stage will depend on the individual client but as a general rule this should be neither rushed or drawn out unnecessarily. Five or six sessions over a period of 2 months or so may be adequate but for a minority of clients the final phase may be longer than this.

Meaning of separation

The final stage of therapy may have different meanings for individual clients and one cannot assume that all clients will find this stage difficult. For some, ambivalence may be dominant. For others, the ending of the therapy and the therapeutic relationship may have little significance but there will be others for whom the emotions of sadness, anger and guilt may be dominant and the meaning of loss and separation needs to be explored. Therapists often appear to have difficulty asking clients about how they feel about therapy ending. If one considers that the therapy is important to the client, and that the therapist is significant to the client, then it is likely that there may be a reaction to the final stage of therapy. Often discussing other endings, such as a personal loss that the client may have experienced and life transitions such as leaving home or a job, can help to introduce both the issue of endings but also highlight that the experience of loss may be both normal and upsetting at the same time.

Many clients who have difficulty with ending therapy may have brought up these issues earlier in therapy. The experience of real or perceived losses in the past is a characteristic of this group of clients. These clients have also experienced difficulties maintaining close relationships. During the main phase of therapy, the therapist is likely to have looked at the assumptions the client makes about why relationships failed and examined the repertoire of social skills available to the client for maintaining relationships. As stated before, improving social relationships is usually a goal of therapy. In addition, the breakdowns in the therapeutic relationship itself are used to illustrate misunderstandings which may arise in relationships and to make explicit some of the normal rules of relationships. Asking the client to think about what problems might be envisaged when the end of treatment approaches and to anticipate difficulties is helpful in highlighting these issues earlier on in treatment.

Keeping goal-directed

When treating a client with a mental disorder such as depression, in the final stage of cognitive therapy, the patient is clearly less symptomatic and is returning to a recognizable 'normal self' state. One of the differences with treating an individual with personality disorder is that 'normal' functioning is the state which treatment is aiming to change. Defining from the outset what the client wants to change is a key characteristic of therapy and if these changes are stated appropriately, and are realistic, then the end-point of therapy will also be clear. The goals of therapy can be re-negotiated as difficulties become more evident during treatment but should not be greatly different from those stated at the beginning. If defined clearly enough to allow for progress to be monitored, the final stage of treatment will largely consist of consolidation and maintenance of these goals. Along with this consolidation of new beliefs and behaviours, the final phase of therapy is about how this different way of being in the world can be continued without the help of the therapist. In order to accomplish this final phase of work, the therapy has to remain goal directed as well as dealing with the issues which may specifically arise as a result of the meaning of termination for the client.

As only so much change can be undertaken during any one therapeutic contract, some clients may need help again in the future. For the client, the awareness of changes accomplished is heightened by the collection of written summaries which have been gathered as treatment has progressed. To mark the transition of ending therapy, it is appropriate to give another summary or letter of what has been achieved by the client and how the difficulties faced have been surmounted. It is likely that some problems will not have resolved fully and the therapist should help the client to acknowledge this and express regret or frustration, if appropriate. This is not uncommon given the long-standing nature of problems that those with personality disorder experience.

The possibility of an increase in self-harm

In the final stage of therapy, those clients who have self-harmed as a means of reducing distressing emotions such as anxiety and frustration, may increase their use of self-harm. This problem is anxiety-provoking for the therapist and often puts the therapist in a dilemma about the pending discharge of the client. For inexperienced therapists, this might lead to them extending the discharge date or even assuming that the therapy has been totally useless. Other therapists may not know what to do when this happens and feel at a loss as to how to proceed. It is important to deal with this behaviour in a problem-focused manner and not avoid it. The meaning behind an increase in self-harm should be gently explored with the client. It is possible that if self-harm has led to expressions of concern from significant others, including the therapist in the past, an increase in self-harm might be purposeful in that it might lead again to the therapist expressing concern for the client. The client may not be entirely aware of this as a motive, but may only be aware of a panic reaction to a sense of being abandoned. Another client might view the therapy ending as confirmation of unworthiness and view the therapeutic relationship as having been a sham and the therapist as being uncaring and uninterested. Others who increase self-harm at the end of therapy may waver a great deal between apparently valuing therapy and acknowledging the gains made whilst, on the other hand, devaluing the whole treatment process, using the self-harm as evidence that they are no better at coping than they were when they first entered therapy. The key point is that the therapist has to understand the meaning of the increase in self-harm and put this in the context of treatment as a whole and the client's difficulties coping with treatment ending.

Frequency of contact in the final stage of therapy

Although it is often helpful to space out appointments during cognitive therapy, to allow clients to practise specific behaviour and schema change techniques, this is more appropriately carried out in the middle phase of therapy. Decreasing contact with the client in the final stages of treatment is usually not helpful and it is not a matter of the client getting used to not having contact with the therapist. As treatment approaches the end, a decreasing frequency of appointments can be easily misinterpreted by some clients. For example, clients may interpret the therapist's behaviour as indicating a loss of interest in them, or that the therapist is being punitive and uncaring. Clients sometimes will articulate that this is evidence that they are unworthy of therapy or that they have been 'bad' patients. If the client has an abandonment schema, increasing the time between the final appointments may increase a sense of abandonment rather than allow the opportunity to work through the meaning of this for the client.

Building up community resources and contacts with others

Community resources which can be accessed by clients with mental health problems exist in most cities and clients can be encouraged to find out about these and explore options at an early stage in therapy. These should not be regarded as replacing therapy when it ends but as an adjunct to treatment and extending the client's opportunities to meet others in a relatively supportive but less intensive environment.

Many clients with personality disorder have impoverished and dysfunctional social relationships and a goal of therapy is to improve the client's social relationships. This might include involving significant others in therapy or building up a client's social skills and confidence to begin new relationships and activities. This helps to reduce the dependency on the therapist. By the end of therapy, clients will ideally have formed some relationships or put in place some purposeful outside activity such as a voluntary job or even paid employment. These relationships may sometimes still be at a relatively fragile stage but ultimately, these are more adaptive and more reality-based in the longer term than a sole relationship with a therapist.

Therapy in action: A case illustration of borderline personality disorder

Jean, a 28-year-old, single, unemployed woman, was referred for cognitive therapy by a Community Mental Health Team. She had been in psychiatric treatment following a serious overdose and had been diagnosed as having a depressive disorder which had partially responded to a combination of medications. She had a lengthy history of self-harm, which included cutting herself and overdosing. Although her self-harm had decreased in the recent past, her psychiatrist was concerned that this behaviour was long-standing and had not been substantially altered as her depression had improved.

Assessment period

Some of the information included here as being part of the initial assessment period was obtained at a later stage of therapy but is mentioned at this point to increase coherence. In addition, details have been altered to protect the patient's identity.

An assessment of Jean's problems and background took place over the first three sessions. It was important not to hurry this as Jean had little idea of what help she wanted but was very distressed. She acknowledged that her self-mutilation was now seriously affecting her physical integrity as her arm was so badly damaged that any further damage might increase the risk of her losing the full use of one of her hands.

Main presenting problems

During the first three sessions, Jean revealed features which were indicative of Borderline personality disorder. As well as recurrent suicidal behaviours and self-mutilation, she reported that she had difficulty with her mood and described herself as being on an emotional roller-coaster, seldom able to maintain any emotional equilibrium. Her antidepressant therapy had helped to stabilize her mood but she continued to feel vulnerable emotionally and she still experienced intense feelings of 'black moods' which lasted for several days at a time. At these times, she thought nothing had changed and that antidepressants had not changed her underlying feeling of desperation and anxiety. She had at various times in her life had eating problems, both starving herself and bingeing, but had never received help for this difficulty. Her current weight was within the normal range and she said she did not have current difficulties with eating, although she was drinking heavily. Roughly once a month, she would consume a bottle or two of wine over a few hours.

Jean had few social contacts and found it hard to make and keep friendships. She was afraid of other people letting her down and said that she thought others were likely to criticize and reject her. She had last worked about four years previously, as a nanny, but had been sacked from this job after an overdose. She said she had not found a job or occupation to suit her and had now given up trying to find work, despite the economic hardship which she faced as a result. She spent most of her time alone in her flat, rarely going out.

Personal history

Jean was the youngest child and only daughter in her family, having two older brothers. She described an unhappy childhood and adolescence. Jean had been brought up in a village in the South of Scotland. When Jean was a baby, her parents had returned to Scotland from abroad to run their own business. Jean had few specific memories of her early childhood. She said she had been lonely as a child and that she had not seen much of her parents as they had been building up their business. She and her brothers had been looked after by a series of *au pairs* and housekeepers, none of whom appeared to stay with the family for long. Her older brothers preferred to play with each other rather than with her. They had been sent off to boarding school when they were 8 whilst she had been kept at home and attended the local school until the age of 11. She had not made many friends at primary school and she had learned to avoid inviting other children home to play as her home life was different from theirs, partly because her parents were not at home and because the local children were not looked after by *au pairs*. Her parents discouraged her from bringing friends home from school as they were often not home until later in the evening. On occasions, she had been to other children's homes after school and was struck by the happy atmosphere in their homes. Her image of other families' lives appeared to be of noise, people chatting and having fun, all of which was far removed from her own rather silent home with an *au pair* sitting drinking coffee in the kitchen or in her room with the door locked to keep Jean out.

Adolescence

She had gone to a boarding school in the South of England and had been miserable for most of that period. She had felt she was being sent away from home because she was a nuisance to her parents. She found it oppressive to be constantly surrounded by others and to have little privacy. She was bullied by some of the older girls at school and made to carry out their chores for them. Nor were the girls her own age any easier to get on with. Jean's mother had discouraged her from paying attention to her appearance and had insisted on plain clothes and sensible shoes. Jean regarded herself as 'a plain Jane' and from an early age she had believed that it was wrong to be vain and to make oneself attractive. At school, how one looked and dressed appeared to be the main focus of conversation. Jean, who had few fashionable clothes, and short curly hair, quickly became an object of ridicule in the dormitory. Girls made fun of her and would offer to dress her up and then laugh at how she looked when she stood awkwardly in front of them.

By her second year at boarding school, she had made some friends. These were not comfortable relationships but characterized by a continuous struggle to be in with the 'right group'. Being thin was a highly desired state at school and several girls developed anorexia. Jean had hidden food during meals in order to lose weight and was seen by the school doctor at the age of 15 because she was underweight and menstruation had stopped. Her parents visited the school and discussion took place about removing her from school. Jean, who was not happy at school but even more unhappy at home, promised to eat and was allowed to continue her education. She forced herself to eat and started to binge on sweets and crisps and put on weight so rapidly that she began vomiting in an attempt to control her weight. This bulimic behaviour, carried out in private, but practised by several other girls, remained in place until she left school. Later, she did develop a friendship with a girl. This friendship was intense and both girls relied a great deal on each other, helping each other with homework and swapping clothes and books. Jean had not seen her friend since leaving school.

University

Jean's school performance improved in her senior years as she felt more settled having made a friendship and she did relatively well in her exams, leaving school with enough qualifications to gain entry to a Scottish university to study modern languages. At university, she had problems coping with a mixed sex environment. At first, she felt ill at ease in tutorials and blushed when she was expected to speak in front of male students. She tried to compensate for her social difficulties by avoiding social activities and achieving high marks in her academic studies. She obtained good marks but she became increasingly isolated from others and concerned about her looks. She began to binge on food and then had periods when she did not eat regularly which resulted in her weight fluctuating.

Her mood began to become depressed and she had frequent suicidal thoughts. Around this time, she also began to scratch her arms. She was not sure why this behaviour began, other than it coincided with her mood being low and anxious. Despite these difficulties, she did well in her first two years and was admitted into honours. She did not go home during summer vacations, preferring to stay in the city. Her parents sent her money and came to see her regularly but made no comment about her not coming home.

At the end of her second year, a fellow classmate persuaded her to go to a party and she met a lecturer there who asked her out. Although awkward and anxious with men, she agreed. By this time she was lonely and had made no close friends except some classmates whom she saw during the day but seldom accompanied to parties or to bars in the evening. Jean's relationship with Simon lasted, off and on, for two and a half years. Simon was older than her by seven years and had also experienced a difficult childhood. She found it hard to describe him other than he was rather moody, quiet and very intelligent. When asked about what the relationship had meant to her, she replied that she had wanted to have a boyfriend as she felt so alone and he made her feel as though she was important, partly because she was dating a lecturer. She had wanted to love Simon but found it difficult to become emotionally involved with him as she was anxious he would be critical of her and reject her.

The relationship eventually became a sexual relationship and she asked him if she could move into his flat. He was initially reluctant to make this commitment, saying that he needed his space to do his work, but by the end of her third year he had agreed. She was, in her own words, desperate to cement the relationship and afraid he would tire of her. Her parents had met this man and her father had commented that he appeared to be a 'decent enough' person. She became pregnant, by mistake, after Christmas of her fourth year, and was so panic stricken by this she told nobody and arranged to have an abortion. By this time, she thought that Simon had lost interest in her and would have regarded the pregnancy as a trap into a permanent relationship. After the abortion, she became depressed and suicidal and took an overdose of antidepressants. Simon, who by this point had found out about the pregnancy and abortion, was kinder than he had ever been initially, but once she was feeling better, he abruptly ended the relationship. This left her feeling desperately alone and suicidal and she took a further overdose. A classmate, hearing of her plight, came to her rescue and offered her a room in her flat which Jean accepted. Although this woman was sympathetic, Jean felt that her story was being spread around her class and that everyone knew that she had taken an overdose and had an abortion. She felt ashamed and humiliated and misunderstood. Her self-harm increased and she became depressed and had to be admitted to hospital for 4 months and was unable to sit her final exams. She was awarded an unclassified honours degree on the basis of her course work.

Early 20s

After her discharge from hospital, her parents took her home. She spent about a year doing very little. Her mood continued to be low and she cut her arms frequently, which she tried to hide from her parents. They, in turn, appeared to ignore her distress and did not talk about her difficulties. Jean once again felt nobody cared about what happened to her and she began to feel rather disengaged from what went on around her. After many months, she began to drink heavily and her mother, finding her unconscious one evening, called in the local doctor who found out she had taken some of her mother's sleeping pills with alcohol. He referred her to a private alcohol problems clinic. She attended there and was told that she was abusing alcohol and given counselling.

Whilst attending the clinic's group sessions, she met Ray, a 50-year-old divorcee. She formed an intense and unstable relationship with him. He wanted to marry her within a month of meeting but she resisted this as she felt she could not trust him. In addition, she felt uncomfortable and anxious when Ray was around but alone and depressed when she was not with him. The relationship continued but was stormy, with Ray continuing to drink too much and arguing with her. She would try to end the relationship, feel alone and empty and would then become self-destructive, drinking and harming herself, and would then plead with Ray to come back to her. He would return to the relationship but be emotionally distant and then if she threatened to end the relationship, he would become charming and conciliatory towards her, all of which resulted in her doubting her judgement and feeling very vulnerable emotionally. She overdosed on many occasions during this relationship, sometimes with the intention of dying. Finally, after several months, Ray left one evening after an argument and then refused to answer her phone calls and letters. She saw his wedding photograph in the newspaper a year later.

Several months after her relationship with Ray came to an end, her parents, without her knowledge, had contacted some friends in London and, without mentioning all Jean's problems, they asked if Jean might have a job as a nanny, looking after their children. This couple agreed and Jean, unsure about what to do next and aware that she was drifting aimlessly, went to London. The couple had three young children and Jean liked looking after them as she seemed to find children easier to get on with than adults.

The first few months in this job passed uneventfully and Jean felt as though she had finally found something to do which she liked, and more importantly, being away from home helped her forget about Ray. However, she made no friends and found the couple she was working with unfriendly towards her. They took her on holiday to look after the children, and her employer's brother, who was there, raped her one night after they had all been drinking heavily. Her employer noticed that she was upset and asked her if she had a problem. She told his wife who immediately implied that Jean was to blame. Jean stole some medication from her and took an overdose. After a brief admission to hospital abroad she was sacked and sent home. Jean then went to live with one of her brothers in London and found that she could not cope with him or his wife as they kept telling her what she should do with her life. She began cutting her arms more, she loathed herself, and had difficulty tolerating her unstable mood state. Her brother appeared to be uncaring and she decided to return to Scotland where she rented a small flat.

Over the next year she saw only her parents, who visited her infrequently. She found it hard to look after herself, her eating became irregular, she was not sleeping well, and she continued to cut herself. She lost interest in her appearance and did not wash regularly. She did not go out, and felt worthless and hopeless. She contacted various telephone helplines and eventually a volunteer worker from a mental health association visited her regularly and tried to get her to attend a group the organization ran for women.

Jean took a serious overdose in the spring of the following year and was referred for a psychiatric assessment. She was diagnosed as being depressed and prescribed antidepressants. Personality disturbance was also noted and a tentative diagnosis of Borderline personality disorder was noted. After a further 9 months she had made a partial recovery in that her sleep and appetite had improved but she was continuing to self-harm and believed herself to be worthless. She was referred for cognitive therapy.

Relevant family history

Jean had described her parents as aloof and as being emotionally distant figures. She said she did not know them well. Her mother was the daughter of a missionary family and had lived abroad for most of her childhood. Jean described her mother as austere, anxious, observing everything that went on and rarely stating an opinion, except a negative one. She did not feel attached to her mother. Her father was warmer than her mother and would occasionally joke with her as a child. She thought that he was hard working and she was sure that he was highly regarded in the local community, where he did much charity and church work.

Jean's mother had suffered from depression, as had her maternal grandmother and aunt. Jean had no knowledge of this until later in therapy when she had asked her mother about mental illness in the family. Her father had no history of psychiatric illness.

Both her brothers had married, although one was now in the process of obtaining a divorce. She did not know her brothers well and felt that they were strangers to her, being older and having been away from home most of her childhood.

Diagnosis

Diagnosis
Dysthymic disorder; major depressive disorder (in remission)
Borderline personality disorder confirmed on formal assessment (DSM-IV)
Features of Avoidant personality disorder

Past diagnosis
Major depressive disorder
Anorexia nervosa (binge eating/purging type)
Alcohol abuse

Initial cognitive formulation

Possible predisposing biological factors
Maternal family history of affective disorder
Anxious, shy child

Significant childhood experience
Emotionally unattached parenting
Little bonding experience with siblings
Experienced self as being different from local children
Interpreted going to boarding school as being 'sent off' because she
   was a nuisance

Significant adolescent and young adult experience
Ridiculed at school for being unattractive
Difficulty making friends within peer group at school and uni-
   versity
Heterosexual relationship characterized by fear of rejection and of
   emotional involvement
Unable to talk to anyone about her pregnancy and abortion
Isolation and social anxiety at university
Sexually assaulted
Difficulty asserting self with parents and others
Self-harming behaviour (overdose, cutting and self-neglect)

Possible core beliefs and dysfunctional assumptions
If I get close to someone, I will be overwhelmed emotionally
I am worthless
I am ugly
Nobody will ever love me
Others are cold, critical, rejecting

Emotional responses
Predominantly depressive or anxious/avoidant

Established problematic behaviours
Self-harm (overdoses and cuts self)
Abuses alcohol
Avoids or is ambivalent of closeness and intimacy
Passive in relationships (even when these are destructive)

Environmental factors
Lives alone and is socially isolated
Family disinterested or potentially will interfere with change

Potential problems in therapy

Likely to have difficulty engaging in treatment as she may be reluctant to trust the therapist and will be afraid of being criticized

Ending of treatment may be problematic as she has few other supports and may become overly dependent on the therapist

Over the next two sessions the above initial formulation was discussed with Jean. The therapist made explicit links with Jean's past and current problems, which were all long-standing. Jean's view of herself and of others was adequately reflected in the core beliefs. There were several aspects of the formulation which particularly made sense to her: Jean agreed that she avoided emotional involvement with others because she had learned that she might be criticized and rejected. In addition, the link between the lack of affection and spontaneity in her childhood and adolescence and her belief that others were emotionally cold made sense to her. With the therapist, links were made between these beliefs and her behaviour. Her lack of experience of affection, her mother's critical stance towards her and being 'sent off' to boarding school had all led her to trying to protect herself from others. She knew she isolated herself from others but she also recognized that this strategy led to her feeling more alone. She was concerned that she would never find anyone who could fulfil her need to be loved. Her more physically destructive behaviours, cutting, overdosing and abusing alcohol, were related to her desire to cut off from strong emotions and thoughts about how useless and worthless she felt about herself.

Once the therapist and Jean had made these links between her behaviour and core beliefs, they discussed how to proceed in therapy. A further five sessions were suggested initially, Jean having had five already. This allowed Jean to commit herself without feeling overwhelmed and allowed progress with this style of therapy to be reviewed. As Jean had relatively serious problems and the level of her personality disturbance was moderately severe, the therapist emphasized behavioural rather than cognitive work for the first phase of treatment. The following treatment plan arose out of the formulation.

Treatment plan

- Sessions 1 to 5
  Assessment and introduction to cognitive model.
  Shared formulation.
  Agree treatment aims.

- Sessions 5 to 10 (concentrate on behavioural change)
  Decrease self-destructive behaviours.
  Increase self-care.
  Review aims and progress.

  Continue with therapy if agreed
- Sessions 11 to 20 (mesh behavioural changes with schema change)
  Work on interpersonal problems.
  Decrease self-destructive behaviours.
  Review and document progress.

  Continue with therapy if agreed
- Sessions 21 to 30 (mesh behavioural changes with schema change)
  Maintain behavioural changes.
  Schema modification continues.
  Review and document progress.
  Negotiate end of treatment date and increase frequency of sessions.

- Sessions 31 to 35
  Work on maintaining behavioural and cognitive changes.
  Work on ending treatment issues.

Sessions 1 to 5: assessment and formulation

Although it is helpful to negotiate a treatment contract which stipulates an expectation about attendance, the therapist decided not to emphasize this in Jean's case. From the initial formulation, it appeared that Jean's past was characterized by others making decisions for her and avoidance, and in order to establish a collaborative relationship, it would be better to inform Jean that the process of therapy would allow her, to some extent, to set the initial pace of therapy. To introduce Jean to the collaborative style of therapy, and to discuss the issue of attendance and control, the following discussion took place.

Th: It seems from what you tell me Jean, that other people have made decisions for you throughout your life and that you may not have thought that you have had a choice about what happens to you. Is that the case?

Jean: (*nods in agreement*)

Th: Do you think that therapy might be like this? Or do you think that you have choices about what happens here?

Jean: I don't know. With the psychiatrist, I went to appointments every month to begin with but I missed several and a nurse came to visit me at home.

Th: I want you to feel that we are working together on your difficulties and this does involve a commitment from you. Would it help if you were able to feel more able to decide what happens in our sessions?

Jean: (*pauses*) Probably.

Th: What would stop you coming?

Jean: (*pause*) I sometimes find it hard to talk about myself.

Th: And that is why you might not attend? (*Jean nods*) Well this therapy is about you, and we will agree what to talk about and what we are working on so that you know what to expect when you are here. I want you to tell me if you are finding it hard to talk about yourself or if you think I'm being pushy. How easy do you think that would be for you?

Jean: Quite difficult.

Th: What if I asked you to decide what we were to talk about each time and if I think something is very important, we can see if you are up to discussing it. If you are finding it too hard, you can say so and I'll agree to stop talking about that. I may bring it up again later in another session, and again you can say if you want to discuss it? Would that make things easier for you? (*Jean nods*) I do want you to come to sessions but only if they are helpful to you. Each time, I'll ask you for feedback about the session and you can tell me what you honestly think about it. Would that be okay with you?

Jean: It sounds okay.

Th: If you don't come for some reason, what would you do?

Jean: I don't know.

Th: Would you want me to phone you to offer you another appointment?

Jean: (*pause*) I'm not sure about that. (*pause*) I'd find that a bit intrusive.

Th: Okay. What would you like to do in that event? How will I know if you want another appointment. Would I write to you with an appointment or would you phone me?

Jean: Could you send another appointment?

Th: Okay. I'll make a note of that.

The next two sessions were spent socializing Jean to the therapy and agreeing the aims of treatment. Priority had to be given to Jean's self-destructive behaviours, particularly cutting herself, and as Jean was realistically concerned about losing the use of her hand, this was agreed without difficulty. Jean, like many with personality disorder, was unsure of what other things she wished to change about herself and it was agreed that the formulation might be useful in guiding her decision about this. As a result, the therapist and Jean put together the initial formulation in the fourth session. The therapist was interested in Jean's conceptualization of her difficulties and found that this was poor. By making links between Jean's current difficulties and her past relationships Jean began to have a better understanding of why she found relationships problematic. Specifically, Jean became aware that her fear of criticism and rejection may have its roots in her childhood. When asked how she wanted to change, Jean became distressed about how she had never been able to have close relationships and how she wanted to have a partner. She became quite angry in the session at this point, stating that she noticed the therapist's wedding ring and how the therapist could have no idea what it was like to be all alone. At this point, the therapist said:

Th: Jean, I can see that you would like to have someone that was close to you. You are very isolated living on your own and it seems from what you have told me that you have had difficulties in relationships. I can see that this is important to you and I can see that this is distressing for you. Do you want to work on this together – trying to improve how you get on with others?

Jean: Yes I do. (*still angry*) But how can I do anything about it? Nobody would ever like me. I'm ugly, useless and I can't cope with relationships. Its fine for you – you're married.

Th: How much do you believe that nobody could ever like you, Jean?

Jean: I try not to think about it. It's too painful to know that I'll always be on my own.

Th: What about Simon? Does that relationship count in your opinion?

Jean: Only a bit. We were both odd ... lost souls together. I was still lonely in that relationship.

Th: But does it count as a relationship albeit in the past?

Jean: No, because it failed.

Th: Jean, just because a relationship fails, does it mean it doesn't count towards our experience in life? (*Jean tentatively shakes her head*) In this therapy, we will try to understand why your relationships have not been successful and what you need to do to improve your relationships with other people. By the end of treatment you may not have an intimate relationship but you may have more ideas about what kind of relationship you would like to have. Can we learn from our failed relationships in your view?

Jean: (*pause*) In theory. But it is too painful for me to contemplate another relationship. I had that disaster with Ray and I don't want to go through that again.

Th: You seem afraid of attempting to have other relationships yet you desperately want to be in one?

Jean: Yes I know.

Th: But you want to have someone close to you? Do you mean a man here?

Jean: Yes, but I can't even have relationships with women.

Th: Would you like us to talk about this later on in therapy? Go over the relationships you have had and see what has happened more clearly and why you are so afraid?

Jean: Yes. But I don't know how to relate to other people. I'm shouting at you and I'm scared you are seeing me as scum ... (*cries*)

Th: (*after some moments*) I can see this upsets you and I am glad you have told me how you feel and how you think I might view you negatively. I know from your history that others have been critical and rejecting of you. We have to work on this together, on the same side. That means that I will be open with you about relationships and ours included. What gives you the impression that I see you as scum?

Jean: You are married and I can't have relationships. That makes me a failure in everyone's eyes and because I push people away, they see me as nasty.

Th: If I am married, do you think that means I cannot understand that other people have problems in relationships?

Jean: No I suppose it doesn't.

Th: Most of the people I see here do not have relationships or are having problems in relationships. In my life outside work, I know many men and women who have problems in relationships. It seems to me that this is normal and that it also causes a lot of distress. Do you now think that I believe those who do not have relationships, or who have problems because they are afraid of being rejected, are scum?

Jean: No.

Th: Shall we work on relationships in our sessions together? We appear to have started on our relationship! (*Both laugh*). I guess it helps to clear the air of misunderstandings when they arise, eh?

Jean: (*Smiles and nods*).

By the end of session 5, the treatment aims were specified as follows:

1. Decrease self-harm behaviours (cutting, overdosing).

2. Increase self-caring (eating regularly, self-presentation, sleep schedule etc.).
3. Monitor alcohol consumption and note how this affects mood.
4. Once self-harm is reduced, and Jean has more control over this, work on establishing and maintaining relationships.

Sessions 5 to 10: concentrate on behavioural change

The overall aims of sessions 5 to 10 were to decrease self-harm behaviours and increase self-care. Jean had not cut her arms since entering therapy but had reported experiencing several strong urges to do so. The main reason for not cutting herself appeared to be Jean's knowledge that this might cause potentially irreparable damage to her arm. The therapist used problem-solving techniques to help Jean explore ways in which she could keep herself safe from harm. Jean managed to generate a list of possible actions she could take to keep herself safe both in the short and longer term. Amongst her most favoured potential solutions were keeping only fixed safety razors in her home and only keeping a small supply of medication at any one time, including paracetamol. She set herself a goal of throwing away the stock of medication which she had hoarded over a year but she would only agree to throw out a little at a time. The therapist agreed this would be an adaptive strategy for Jean even though she would have preferred Jean to make the medication less accessible. Jean would not agree to getting rid of all non-essential medication and said she 'needed' to know it was there if she got desperate. Given that the therapist was trying to ensure a collaborative relationship with Jean and was encouraging Jean to make decisions for herself, this appeared both appropriate and realistic. The therapist emphasized that Jean had options available to her, including harming herself, and that therapy aimed to increase Jean's ability to look after herself in a positive way.

It was increasingly evident from further discussion with Jean that she harmed herself in response to certain mood states and situations. Jean would cut herself after a period of being intensely upset, and when worn out and exhausted, she would begin to feel disengaged from everything around her. In this state, she would cut herself in order to feel physical pain as opposed to mental pain. The sight of her own blood she said had a calming effect on her and she would set about cleaning the wound or going to an Accident and Emergency Department if necessary. She hated attending hospital to have stitches as she found the attitude of the staff humiliating and she felt that they did not understand her. In the recent past she had to attend hospital as her arm was badly damaged and (fortunately) she wanted to avoid this eventuality.

A plan was agreed with Jean to help her to avoid getting to the stage of being worn out and exhausted and cutting. First, as stated above, she agreed to only having safety razors in the house. She was asked to explore ways of not getting overly distressed and disengaged. She was beginning to find talking about problems more helpful, but as the therapist was likely to be unavailable sometimes, other ways of managing her distress had to be found. She eventually decided to phone the male nurse who came to visit her, and arranged to do this with his permission. She told the nurse that she might not be able to talk at these times but asked if he would just let her be on the phone for a while so that she felt his presence during these times of high distress. Other members of nursing staff were briefed that Jean may call in distress and that their role was to listen if she wanted to talk and just be there for a while on the phone if she did not want to talk. This strategy worked well and Jean used this several times over the next 6 months until she no longer needed to do so. In addition, the therapist encouraged Jean to find other strategies which were more self-reliant. After several sessions, Jean decided on several which had worked in the past and which she would be able to utilize system-atically. These involved going to bed if very upset and having 'time out', wrapping herself in a blanket and lying on the couch, and playing music which she found soothing and which would not lower her mood further.

A common situation which led to Jean being distressed was her mother phoning her. She phoned once a week on average and the conversation was almost identical each time. Jean was asked what she had been doing, and as she had very little to report, her mother usually said very little and after several long silences, they both said goodbye. Jean thought that her mother called her out of duty rather than concern and that her silence implied criticism of Jean's lifestyle. Jean told her mother very little, mostly because she thought her mother was uninterested. Her mother knew she had attended a psychiatrist for depression but Jean had not told her about attending a cognitive therapist. When asked why she thought her mother was critical, Jean recounted several episodes in her childhood when her mother had made Jean stand in front of her and tell her what she had done wrong. Her mother heard these accounts in silence and then asked Jean what she was to do with her. Jean was then usually punished by being kept in her room or made to do extra chores around the house. Jean also said that her mother would enter her bedroom at night when she was in bed and stare at her, saying nothing and then leave. These episodes had frightened Jean as a child as she could not understand why her mother behaved in this way. Jean equated her mother's silence with these episodes in her child-hood and interpreted them as her mother regarding her as a being bad, a nuisance, and at worst, a worthless individual.

Given this information, it was understandable that Jean thought her mother regarded her negatively. Jean was asked if there were positive memories of her mother and little evidence of happier episodes emerged. Jean was at a loss to explain or reframe her mother's behaviour. The therapist speculated that her mother had been unwell, perhaps depressed, or had worries of her own which Jean did not know of and which she was unable to resolve. Such speculations were not accepted by Jean, but she did agree she did not know her mother well nor did she wish to know her better, as she found her so negative. Jean was asked if she thought that her mother's regular phone calls could be an indication of caring but Jean found this hard to accept. After looking at several options for managing the phone calls, Jean agreed to take more control over the phone calls and initiate the calls herself. She planned to phone every ten days or so and, as she was paying for the calls, she could reasonably keep them short. She also thought it would be helpful if she could ask her mother questions about what she had been doing rather than have all the attention placed on her. This increase in assertiveness was highlighted by the therapist.

Jean was asked to keep a record of her alcohol consumption and how this affected her mood but did not do so. The therapist systematically enquired about this each session and a relatively clear pattern emerged. Jean was not consuming alcohol on most days but if she did drink, she consumed at least a bottle of wine. This usually sent her to sleep early but her sleep was then disturbed later in the night and her mood was low over the next two days. The therapist kept a record of this and gave a copy to Jean but other than this there was no intervention planned and sessions focused on reducing other forms of self-harm. Jean was also asked about her eating and agreed to try to eat regular meals and nutritional food.

At the tenth session, Jean did not think she had made any progress. She still felt she was worthless. The therapist, who had kept a record of her agreed tasks, asked about how Jean viewed progress in these. Jean acknowledged that she had started phoning her mother and asking about what she had done. Jean had discovered that asking about her father was more productive as her mother did not like speaking about herself. This had helped Jean cope better with her contact with her mother. She had not cut herself for several months and had put into operation some of the agreed strategies and found those helpful. The therapist summarized the changes as being mainly in Jean's behaviour and asked Jean if she still believed she was worthless. An explanation was given about how the therapist would not expect Jean to feel differently about herself as she had thought this way since she was a child. Changing her behaviour in such a short period was a surprise to Jean and she was asked to enter into the next phase of therapy, which would involve examining the way she thought of herself and others as well as behaviour change. Jean agreed to another ten sessions and it was acknowledged that she was now more confident about being able to speak about herself in sessions.

Sessions 11 to 20: mesh behavioural changes with schema change

This phase of therapy took place over approximately 3 months. The focus was on Jean's view of herself and others as reflected in her core beliefs and the behavioural strategies which arose from these beliefs. The therapeutic task was to begin to modify Jean's core beliefs by establishing alternative more adaptive beliefs and behavioural strategies.

Most of the cognitive work took place within sessions, with Jean attempting to change her behaviour towards herself and others in the time between sessions. The belief that others were cold, critical and rejecting became the main focus of sessions as this was central to Jean's avoidant behaviour. In tandem, Jean carried out behavioural tasks which were designed to provide information to evaluate her core beliefs. From the first 10 sessions, it was evident that Jean believed that people would be critical of her and that even if someone appeared to be kind or warm, this was likely to be temporary and eventually she would find them to be cold towards her, critical and rejecting.

Several cognitive techniques were used to explore the adaptiveness and veracity of her beliefs but the one which was used throughout treatment was the continuum. Jean was asked what statement she would put at the opposite end of a continuum that had at one pole the statement 'Everyone is rejecting'. After some discussion, Jean decided on a uni-directional continuum with the statement 'Some people are reasonably friendly'. This was phrased in this way to try to force Jean to begin to evaluate individuals in terms of friendliness as she clearly only attended to negative aspects of relationships, and ignored any friendly overtures from others.

The continuum was written as shown in Figure 12.1.

Initially, Jean believed that this statement was true 0%, that is, nobody was friendly towards her. Jean was then asked to detail the

Some people are reasonably friendly

0%   50%   100%

Figure 12.1   Jean's uni-directional continuum

way in which she might judge someone to be friendly. The therapist also took an active role in this discussion and listed some of the ways she thought others displayed friendliness. Jean was not asked to accept the therapist's view but to keep an open mind and develop her observation skills. After a few sessions, Jean listed some of the following characteristics of friendly behaviour in others – smiling, laughing with someone, looking at someone directly, listening attentively, standing quite close etc. Armed with this information, Jean was asked to observe other people in social situations and chose to go to a cafe near her home to do so. This task was not easy for Jean as she had become used to staying at home on her own and going to a public place was mildly anxiety-provoking for her. None the less she carried out the assignment and reported that she had been able to observe friendly behaviour in other people. Whether or not others could be friendly towards her remained unanswered. She was asked to evaluate her contacts with shopkeepers, neighbours, and those she came into contact with. By session 14, she had some evidence that some people were friendly towards her but they were strangers to her and not people she wanted to have as friends. In order to test out that she might be liked by others who might become friends, she had to find a way of meeting people who might share her interests. As she had studied modern languages at university, Jean suggested that she might want to maintain her interest in this and she was set the task of finding out how she might do this as well as other ways of meeting people.

This task proved to be too great and Jean felt overwhelmed at the idea that she had to meet people. Jean telephoned the therapist saying that she wanted to harm herself and was feeling very low and had been drinking. She was instructed to keep herself safe by lying on the couch and not cutting and she was asked to remind herself that she had experience that these feelings would pass. The therapist asked Jean to stop drinking alcohol and try to go to sleep. The following session was brought forward and the therapist saw her again two days later. Jean had not cut herself and was feeling less depressed but still very overwhelmed. It was agreed that she may have taken on too great a task and that breaking the task down further might be helpful. Jean still felt she wanted to cut herself and was asked how she might keep herself safe from harm. She suggested that she would not drink alcohol as this clearly made her mood and thoughts worse. The therapist then encouraged Jean to think of other strategies. Finally, they agreed Jean would take 'time out' on the couch, not drink alcohol, and make sure she was eating properly and not skipping meals and would also try to go out of her house at least once a day.

By the following session, Jean was feeling more in control and the task of meeting people was reviewed and broken down into less anxiety-provoking goals so that Jean would not feel overwhelmed. She agreed the following tasks to be carried out over a month. The aim was to allow Jean opportunities to meet others and to evaluate the degree to which they were friendly.

1. Phone language centre to enquire about classes.
2. Visit language centre to enquire about conversation classes.
3. Contact language school to find out about tutoring children in French and Spanish.
4. Offer to help elderly neighbour with her shopping.
5. Invite younger neighbour in for coffee.
6. Ask (local) brother's children out to cinema.

In addition, the therapist began working systematically on Jean's belief that she was worthless. Having succeeded in not cutting herself and reducing her alcohol consumption, Jean was surprised at herself but did not appear to value this change in her behaviour. The therapist was positive about Jean having prevented more damage to her arm and asked the following questions:

Th: Was it hard for you to resist harming yourself?
Jean: (*pause*) It was very difficult. I've always cut myself at these times.
Th: You did well not to do it again, especially when it was such a difficult time for you. How did you manage, Jean?
Jean; I tried to wait till the feelings passed and they did pass.
Th: Did you do anything else? What about not drinking alcohol?
Jean: I knew I shouldn't drink any more. It just makes me feel worse and in a state.
Th: It sounds as if you managed to avert the crisis and then went on to look after yourself?
Jean: Yeah. I have to if I want to get out of this hole.
Th: What does looking after yourself mean to you, Jean?
Jean: I'm not sure ... I suppose I want to feel better about me – not totally worthless.

Old belief: I am worthless

0%	50%	100%

I have never done anything useful in my life	I am always doing things which are very helpful to others
0	100

I am completely stupid	I am extremely intelligent
0	100

I am ugly	I am very beautiful
0	100

I am socially inept	I am very socially skilled
0	100

Figure 12.2   Jean's criterion continuum for an old belief

Th: So where would you be if we think about a continuum 'I am worth it?' Do you rate yourself 0% or do you think you did better than that?

Jean: Maybe a bit along from 0% – maybe 10%.

Over the next few weeks, Jean managed to accomplish some but not all of the tasks set and with each new encounter noted how she thought others had responded to her. She was still cautious about interpreting other people's behaviour as being friendly but could acknowledge that not everyone was unfriendly. Having coffee with her neighbour went well and her elderly neighbour turned out to be very friendly and had invited Jean to have tea with her. She found out that conversational classes at an advanced level were available after summer and she had tentatively enrolled.

Jean was gathering as much evidence as possible about whether or not others could be friendly towards her and evidence that would refute the idea that she was worthless. Criteria were developed for her belief that she was worthless so that different types of evidence could be evaluated (see Figure 12.2).

During sessions, work was carried out on Jean's core beliefs. Initially, no difference had been noted in how Jean perceived herself as she tended to dismiss evidence and was not able to change the degree to which she believed she was worthless. By consistent challenging of her belief, and using the behavioural evidence she was gathering, she gradually began to consistently shift the degree to which she believed that she was a worthy individual whom others might like to be friendly towards. It was this consistent and systematic gathering of evidence and challenging of her view of others and self which appeared to shift her beliefs and this, in turn, allowed her to become more confident in managing the behavioural tasks.

By session 20, Jean had made progress and wanted to continue with the same work and to talk more about her past, to which the therapist agreed.

Sessions 21 to 30: mesh behavioural changes with schema change

Jean's behavioural and schema work continued over the next ten sessions, with Jean gathering as much evidence as possible about whether or not others could be friendly towards her and if she had evidence against the belief that she was worthless. In addition, some parts of sessions were devoted to talking about Jean's past. The main topic was her relationship with her mother. Her brother's wife had told her that her mother had suffered from depression. When Jean asked more about this, she revealed that her mother had been depressed around the births of all three children and that she had found it very difficult to cope and that housekeepers and *au pairs* had been employed to help look after the children and allow her mother to recover from depression. Her sister-in-law had suffered from post-natal depression and had been told of her mother-in-law's depression at that time. Although this piece of information helped Jean to understand her mother's behaviour, she was increasingly resentful of how she had been ignored as a child and sent off to school. She believed that her mother's behaviour had resulted in her feeling worthless and guarding herself against others.

It was obvious to Jean that she could not change the past, and she was made aware, through further discussion, that she had begun the task of changing how she felt about herself and others and did not have to follow on with the legacy of her childhood. By this point in therapy, she had collected a dossier of evidence to suggest that she had value and that some people might be friendly towards her, even if she had no special relationship with anyone. Further work was done exploring her childhood, using the historical test of schema, to evaluate her belief that others had been cold and critical towards her. This work was fruitful in altering Jean's view of her childhood and she was able to recall episodes of others being supportive and kind, particularly her grandmother and her father. An extract is presented in Figure 12.3.

As the thirtieth session approached, the therapist began to discuss ending therapy with Jean. By this time, the summer was over and Jean had been attending French and Spanish conversation classes, which she had found enjoyable although initially daunting as it had involved meeting other people. She had found it hard to answer questions about what she did as she had no job and she had assumed that others would evaluate her negatively. This, and the thought of ending therapy, had precipitated another crisis in which Jean had cut herself. She had regretted having harmed herself and thought that all her progress had been for nothing. She had phoned the therapist and talked this through and having challenged her view that she had made no progress, despite cutting again, Jean had managed to put the episode behind her and move on.

Sessions 31 to 35: the final sessions

The final five sessions were used to evaluate the progress made and to discuss ways in which Jean could continue with the work she had begun. These last five sessions took place approximately weekly to enable issues to do with ending therapy to be discussed fully within sessions. Jean was not confident about her ability to cope without therapy or the therapist. She believed that she would relapse without regular sessions and she said that she would miss seeing the therapist.

In reviewing her progress, Jean acknowledged that she had done well to cut down her alcohol consumption, had reduced the degree to which she self-harmed and had managed to establish regular contact with her neighbours and with others through her French and Spanish conversation classes. Her mood was less volatile, and although she became distressed at times, these episodes were more contained and shorter in duration. Her contact with the psychiatric team continued on an infrequent basis and the male nurse had agreed to continue to see Jean, when necessary, for crisis manage-ment. Her view of herself and of others had been altered in the sense that these core beliefs were now less rigid and more flexible, and she was aware that at times when she was either anxious or low she continued to ignore or distort evidence that would be contrary

---

Evidence that supports the old belief

Belief: other people were cold and critical

Age 8 to 12 years

My mother never seemed to show any interest in me

My mother used to tell me she did not know what to do with me if I was bad

The *au pairs* we had at this time did not play with me

At boarding school, girls ridiculed my looks and clothes

Evidence that supports a new belief

New belief: other people were sometimes supportive and kind

Age 8 to 12 years

Girls at my local school used to invite me to their homes

The teachers praised my work

One of the *au pairs* used to let me use her make-up and try on her clothes

At boarding school, another new girl helped me with maths homework

My father used to take me on walks in the countryside every weekend

My father used to play with me and my brothers during the school holidays

My grandmother used to give me sweets when my mother wasn't watching

My grandmother used to read stories to me at night and tell me jokes

---

Figure 12.3   Extract from Jean's historical test of a schema

to her original core beliefs. She needed to continue with the behavioural changes she had made.

The end of therapy was difficult for Jean. She had managed to form a good relationship with her therapist and had been able to trust her.

The therapist asked what ending therapy meant to Jean. She said it signified the end of their relationship and she was sad about that and she asked if she would be able to contact the therapist if she needed to. At this point, the therapist acknowledged that she was also sad that the relationship was coming to an end. The therapist asked Jean if she thought that she was being rejected to which she answered that ending the therapy had brought some of the 'old' feelings and thoughts about rejection to the fore and admitted that she had struggled with these feelings for several weeks, knowing that the end was to be expected as they had often talked about ending therapy in sessions. The therapist pointed out that therapy had to come to an end and that it was understandable that Jean should feel this way. Indeed, given Jean's past history, she had done well to recognize the feelings and thoughts. She asked Jean how she was managing to deal with these feelings and thoughts. Jean said she had felt anxious about the end of therapy and had thought about taking an overdose. She had looked at the dossier of information she had gathered in treatment and, although she had remained anxious, had been able to counter her thoughts about coping on her own. She had evidence that other people liked her and that she was not worthless and did not want to deliberately diminish the progress she had made by over-dosing. She also said she wondered if the therapist would extend the treatment if she overdosed. She added with a wry smile that the therapist had concentrated on what Jean could do to improve her life and would be unlikely to be swayed by such an action. The therapist agreed with Jean's assessment of the situation, emphasizing that the overdosing in itself was not what therapy had concentrated on but Jean's strengths in being able to lead a better quality of life by looking after herself in a more adaptive way. She told Jean that she would be interested in how Jean fared in the future and if, after some time passed, Jean required further help, she could be assessed again.

Prior to the last session, the therapist gave Jean a letter summarizing what had happened in therapy and detailing the formulation which they had jointly endorsed. The letter pointed out Jean's strengths and what she had achieved during therapy and how she had learned to look after herself. On the last session, Jean was tearful but interpreted this as being normal after such a length of time in therapy. She was not particularly anxious about her future or her ability to cope without therapy as she said that she had to try to do this if she was to develop a better life for herself. The final session ended with the therapist wishing Jean well for the future.

Appendix

What are core beliefs?

Core beliefs are strong beliefs that you may hold about yourself or other people. You do not question these beliefs, they simply seem to be true. Core beliefs are not always obvious and you may not always be aware of a core belief. However, these beliefs are very powerful and when your thoughts and emotions appear to be extremely negative and overwhelming, it is likely that a core belief is dominating the way in which you are viewing yourself and the world around you. It is likely that these beliefs develop in childhood, when you are too young to be able to evaluate whether or not they are true.

For example, Jenny had a belief that she was bad. She said that she had always thought this about herself and that this was just how she was. When her therapist got to know her better, it appeared that she had thought this way since she was a child. She had been brought up by an aunt who had badly beaten her as a child. Rather than think that her aunt was cruel, she thought that she was being punished for something that she had done. The only way she could make sense of these beatings as a child was to believe she had done something wrong. As she grew older, other experiences were interpreted to fit in with this belief. When she was told off in school by teachers, when her schoolmates did not want to play with her, when she never had any boys interested in her as a teenager, she believed that she was bad and that no one could possibly think well of her. She believed this to such an extent that when something positive did happen to her, such as being invited to play with someone, or when she was older, when a young man asked her out, she thought that he was just being nice to her because he felt sorry for her. She believed that if he got to know her well, he would also be able to see that she was not worthy of his affection or attention.

Like Jenny, you may hold a deep and unshakeable belief about yourself or others. It seems that these beliefs are so strong that information is systematically distorted to fit the belief.

How can cognitive therapy help?

In therapy we will examine some of the core beliefs that you hold about yourself and others. It will take time to change such strong beliefs. We will help you to evaluate and weaken these beliefs, and help you to build more adaptive new beliefs. These powerful beliefs are also likely to affect the way in which you behave and cognitive therapy will also enable you to make changes in your behaviour which we hope will improve the quality of your life.

Formulation

Why has the client come
  for help now?

Childhood environment
  and significant early
  experiences

Problematic behaviours

Interpersonal difficulties

Core beliefs about:
Self

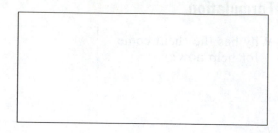

Others

Dominant emotions

Describe any specific
problems with
self-regulation?

Historical test of schema

Evidence that supports the old belief
State old belief:

Age ___ to ___ years

Evidence that supports a new belief
State new belief:

Age ___ to ___ years

References

Akiskal, H.S., Yerevanian, B.I., Davis, G.C. *et al.* (1985) The nosological status of borderline personality: clinical and poly-somnographic study. *American Journal of Psychiatry*, **142**, 192–198.

American Psychiatric Association (1980) *Diagnostic and Statistical Manual of Mental Disorders* (3rd edn) (DSM-III). APA.

American Psychiatric Association (1994) *Diagnostic and Statistical Manual of Mental Disorders* (4th edn)(DSM-IV). APA.

Beck, A.T., Freeman, A. and Associates (1990) *Cognitive Therapy of Personality Disorders.* The Guilford Press.

Beck, A.T., Rush, J., Shaw, B. and Emery, G. (1979) *Cognitive Therapy of Depression.* The Guilford Press.

Bernstein, D.P.; Kasapis, C.; Bergman, A. *et al.* (1997) Assessing Axis II disorders by informant interview. *Journal of Personality Disorders,* **11,** 158–167.

Blackburn, I.M. and Davidson, K.M. (1995) *Cognitive Therapy for Depression and Anxiety: a Practitioner's Guide* (2nd rev. edn). Blackwell Scientific.

Blackburn, I.M., Eunson, K.M. and Bishop, S. (1986) A two year naturalistic follow-up of depressed patients treated with cognitive therapy, pharmacotherapy, and a combination of both. *Journal of Affective Disorders,* **10**, 67–75.

Brown, G. R. and Anderson, B. (1991) Psychiatric morbidity in adult clients with childhood histories of sexual and physical abuse. *American Journal of Psychiatry*, **148**, 55–61.

Burke Draucher, C. (1992) *Counselling Survivors of Childhood Sexual Abuse.* Sage Publications.

Clark, L.A. (1993) *Manual for the Schedule for Nonadaptive and Adaptive Personality*. University of Minnesota Press.

Cloninger, C.R. (1987) A systematic method for clinical description and classification of personality variants: a proposal. *Archives of General Psychiatry*, **44**, 576–588.

Costa, P.T. and McCrae, R.R. (1992) *NEO-PI-R: Professional Manual. Revised NEO Personality Inventory (NEO-PI-R) and NEO Five Factor Inventory (NEO-FFI)*. Psychological Assessment Resources, Inc.

Davidson, K.M. and Tyrer, P. (1996) Cognitive therapy for antisocial and borderline personality disorders: single case series. *British Journal of Clinical Psychology*, **35**, 413–429.

Deary, I. and Power, M.J. (1998) Normal and abnormal personality. In: *Companion to Psychiatric Studies* (6th edn) (Johnstone, E.C., Freeman, C.P.L. and Zealley, A.K., eds). Churchill Livingstone, pp. 565–596.

Dowson, J.H. and Grounds, A.T. (1995) *Personality Disorders: Recognition and Clinical Management*. Cambridge University Press.

Ellis, T. E. and Newman, C. F. (1996) *Choosing to Live: How to Defeat Suicide through Cognitive Therapy*. New Harbinger Publications.

Evans, M.D., Hollon, S.D., DeRubeis, R.J. *et al.* (1992) Differential relapse following cognitive therapy and pharmacotherapy for depression: singly and in combination. *Archives of General Psychiatry*, **49**, 802–808.

Feinstein, A.R. (1970) The pre-therapeutic classification of co-morbidity in chronic disease. *Journal of Chronic Diseases*, **23**, 455–468.

Girolamo, G. and Reich, J.H. (1993) *Personality Disorders. Epidemiology of Mental Disorders and Psychosocial Problems*. WHO.

Greenberger, D. and Padesky, C. A. (1995) *Mind over Mood. A Cognitive Therapy Treatment Manual for Clients*. The Guilford Press.

Hall, L. and Lloyd, S. (1993) *Surviving Child Sexual Abuse*. Falmer Press.

Hollon, S.D., DeRubeis, R.J., Evans, M.D. *et al.* (1992) Cognitive therapy and pharmacotherapy for depression: singly and in combination. *Archives of General Psychiatry*, **49**, 774–781.

Hyler, S. (1994) *Personality Diagnostic Questionnaire PDQ-4*. New York State Psychiatric Institute.

Hyler, S., Reider, R. and Spitzer, R. (1983) *Personality Diagnostic Questionnaire PDQ*. New York State Psychiatric Institute.

Hyler, S., Reider, R., Williams, J.B.W. *et al.* (1988) Personality diagnostic questionnaire: development and preliminary results. *Journal of Personality Disorders*, **2**, 229–237.

Jackson, H. (1998) The assessment of personality disorder: selected issues and directions. In: *Cognitive Psychotherapy of Psychotic and Personality Disorders* (Perris, C. and McGorry, P.D., eds). John Wiley and Sons, pp. 293–314.

Jackson, D.N. and Livesley, W.J. (1995) Possible contributions from personality assessment to the classification of personality disorders. In: *The DSM-IV Personality Disorders. Diagnosis and Treatment of Mental Disorders* (Livesley, W.J., ed.). The Guilford Press, pp. 459–481.

Kabat-Zinn, J., Massion, A.O., Kristeller, J. *et al.* (1992) Effectiveness of a meditation-based stress reduction programme in the treatment of anxiety disorders. *American Journal of Psychiatry*, **149**, 936–943.

Klein, M.H. (1993) Issues in the assessment of personality disorders. *Journal of Personality Disorders,* Suppl **1**, 18–33.

Lenzenweger, M.F., Loranger, A.W., Korfine, L. and Neff, C. (1997) Detecting personality disorders in a nonclinical population. Application of a 2-stage procedure for case identification. *Archives of General Psychiatry*, **54**, 345–351.

Linehan, M.M. (1993a) *Cognitive-Behavioral Treatment of Borderline Personality Disorder*. The Guilford Press.

Linehan, M.M. (1993b) *Skills Training Manual for Treating Borderline Personality Disorder*. The Guilford Press.

Linehan, M.M., Armstrong, H.E., Suarez, A. *et al.* (1991) Cognitive-behavioral treatment for chronically parasuicidal borderline patients. *Archives of General Psychiatry*, **48**, 1060–1064.

Linehan, M.M., Heard, H.L. and Armstrong, H.E. (1993) Naturalistic follow-up of a behavioural treatment for chronically parasuicidal borderline patients. *Archives of General Psychiatry*, **50**, 971–974.

Livesley, W.J. and Jackson, D. (in press) *Manual for the Dimensional Assessment of Personality Pathology – Basic Questionnaire*. Sigma Press.

Loranger, A.W. (1990) The impact of DSM-III on diagnosing practice in a university hospital. *Archives of General Psychiatry*, **47**, 672–675.

Loranger, A.W., Susman, V.L., Oldham, J.M. and Russakoff, L.M. (1987) The Personality Disorder Examination: a preliminary report. *Journal of Personality Disorders*, **1**, 1–13.

Loranger, A.W., Sartorius, N., Andreoli, A. *et al.* (1994) The international personality disorder examination. *Archives of General Psychiatry*, **51**, 215–224.

Maser, J.D. and Cloninger, C.R. (1990) Comorbidity of anxiety and mood disorders: introduction and overview. In: *Comorbidity of Mood and Anxiety Disorders* (Maser, J.D. and Cloninger, C.R., eds). American Psychiatric Press Inc., pp 3–12.

Mendel, P.M. (1995) *The Male Survivor – the Impact of Sexual Abuse*. Sage Publications.

Millon, T., Millon, C. and Davis, R.D. (1994) *Millon Clinical Multiaxial Inventory-III*. National Computer Systems.

Murphy, G.E., Simons, A.D., Wetzel, R.D. and Lustman, P.J. (1984) Cognitive therapy and pharmacotherapy, singly and together, in the treatment of depression. *Archives of General Psychiatry*, **41**, 33–41.

Nestadt, G., Romanoski, A.J., Chanal, R. *et al.* (1990) An epidemiological study of histrionic personality disorder. *Psychological Medicine*, **20**, 413–422.

Nestadt, G., Romanoski, A.J., Brown, C.H. *et al.* (1991) DSM-III compulsive personality disorder: an epidemiological survey. *Psychological Medicine*, **21**, 461–471.

Padesky, C.A. (1994) Schema change processes in cognitive therapy. *Clinical Psychology and Psychotherapy*, **1**, 267–278.

Persons, J.B. and Bertagnolli, A. (1994) Cognitive-behavioural treatment of multiple-problem clients: application to personality disorders. *Clinical Psychology and Psychotherapy*, **1**, 279–285.

Pfohl, B., Blum, N., Zimmerman, M. and Stangl, D. (1989) *Structured Interview for DSM-III-R Personality (SIDP-R)*. University of Iowa.

Riech, J., Yates, W. and Nduaguba, M. (1989) Prevalence of DSM-III personality disorders in the community. *Social Psychiatry and Psychiatric Epidemiology*, **24**, 12–16.

Ryle, A.(1997) The structure and development of borderline personality disorder: a proposed model. *British Journal of Psychiatry*, **170**, 82–87.

Shea, M.T., Pilkonis, P.A., Beckham, E. *et al.* (1990) Personality disorders and treatment outcome in the NIMH treatment of depression collaborative research program. *American Journal of Psychiatry*, **147**, 711–718.

Shea, M.T., Elkin, I., Imber, S.D. *et al.* (1992) Course of depressive symptoms over follow-up: findings from the National Institute of Mental Health Treatment of Depression Collaborative Program. *Archives of General Psychiatry*, **49**, 782–787.

Simons, A.D., Murphy, G.E., Levine ,J.L. and Wetzel, R.D. (1986) Cognitive therapy and pharmacotherapy for depression: Sustained improvement over one year. *Archives of General Psychiatry*, **43**, 43–48.

Spitzer, R.L., Williams, J.B.W., Gibbon, M. and First, M. (1990) *User's Guide for the Structured Clinical Interview for DSM-III-R*. American Psychiatric Association.

Strack, S. and Lorr, M. (1997) Invited essay: the challenge of differential normal and disordered personality. *Journal of Personality Disorder*, **11**, 105–122.

Swatrz, M., Blazer, D., George, L. and Winfield, I. (1990) Estimating the prevalence of borderline personality disorder in the community. *Journal of Personality Disorders*, **4**, 257–272.

Turkat, I.D. and Maisto, S.A. (1985) Personality disorders: application of the experimental method to the formulation and modification of personality disorders. In: *Clinical Handbook of Psychological Disorders: a Step by Step Treatment Manual* (Barlow D.H., ed.). The Guilford Press, pp 502–570.

Tyrer P. (1988) Management of personality disorder In: *Personality Disorder Reviewed* (Tyrer, P., ed.). Heinemann.

Tyrer, P., Alexander, J. and Ferguson, B. (1988) Personality Assessment Schedule (PAS). In: *Personality Disorders: Diagnosis, Management and Course* (Tyrer, P., ed.). Wright, pp. 140–167.

Tyrer, P. *et al.* (2000) *Personality Disorders: Diagnosis, Management and Course*. Butterworth-Heinemann.

Weissman, M.M. (1993) The epidemiology of personality disorder: a 1990 update. *Journal of Personality Disorders*, **7**, 44–62.

Weissman, A.N. and Beck, A.T. (1978) Development and validation of the dysfunctional attitude scale. *Paper presented at the annual meeting of the Association for the Advancement of Behavior Therapy*. Chicago.

Widiger, T.A. (1992) Categorical versus dimensional classification: implications from and for research. *Journal of Personality Disorder*, **6**, 287–300.

Widiger, T.A. and Corbitt, E.M. (1995) Antisocial personality disorder. In *The DSM-IV Personality Disorders. Diagnosis and Treatment of Mental Disorders* (Livesley, W.J., ed.). The Guilford Press.

Widiger, T.A. and Costa, P.T. (1994) Personality and personality disorders. *Journal of Abnormal Psychology*, **103**, 78–91.

World Health Organization (1992a) *The ICD-10 Classification of Mental and Behavioural Disorders: clinical descriptions and diagnostic guidelines*. WHO.

World Health Organization (1992b) *International Statistical Classifi-*

cation of Diseases and Related Health Problems, 10th revision. WHO.

Young, J.E. (1990) *Cognitive Therapy for Personality Disorders: a Schemas-focused Approach.* Professional Resource Exchange, Inc.

Young, J.E. and Brown, G. (1990) *Schema questionnaire.* Unpublished manuscript.

Young, J.E. and Lindemann, M.D. (1992) An integrative schema-focused model for personality disorders. *Journal of Cognitive Psychotherapy,* **6**, 11–23.

Zimmerman, M. (1994) Diagnosing personality disorders: a review of issues and research models. *Archives of General Psychiatry,* **51**, 225–245.

Zimmerman, M. and Coryell, W.H. (1990) Diagnosing personality disorders in the community: a comparison of self-report and interview measures. *Archives of General Psychiatry,* **47**, 527–531.

Index

Activity schedules, 84
Affective disorder, 3
Affective responses, 61
Aggression, 83, 86–9, 90, 108–9
Alcohol abuse, 83, 84–6, 87
Anger, 83, 86–9, 90
   measurement scale, 108–9
Antisocial personality disorder, 6,
   81–2
   behavioural strategies, 17
   cognitive model, 17
   core beliefs, 17
   prevalence, 10
   sex differences, 10
   treatment, 82–93
Appointments, 36
Assertiveness training, 89–90
Assignments, 42
Assumptions, 59–60
Automatic thoughts, 24, 31, 59, 65
Avoidant personality disorder, 7–8
   prevalence, 11

Behaviour, programmed, 15–16
Behaviour change, 32, 39–40
Behaviour problems, 14, 16, 17,
   54–5, 65–8

Behaviour therapy, 13, 83–93,
   96–105
Behavioural contracts, 90–2
Beliefs, *see* Core beliefs
Borderline personality disorder,
   3–4, 7, 12, 94, 95
   behavioural strategies, 17
   case illustration, 121–44
   childhood sexual abuse, 105–6
   cognitive model, 17
   core beliefs, 17
   emotional instability, 53
   prevalence, 11
   treatment, 13, 94–106

Case illustration, 121–44
Change measurement, 107–12
Childhood experiences, 52–3, 54,
   64
   sexual abuse, 105–6
Classification systems, 4–5, 9
Client assessment, 46–9
Client feedback, 41–2
Client–therapist relationship,
   27–30, 36–7, 41, 49–50, 63,
   117–18
Clinical interviews, 2–3
Clinical supervision, 45

Cognitive analytical therapy, 13
Cognitive biases, 24
Cognitive models, 15–21
Cognitive processing errors, 24
Cognitive theory of emotional
    disorders, 24–5
Cognitive therapy, 13, 14, 17, 22–
    45
  assessing suitability for, 48
  assignments, 42
  case illustration, 121–44
  ending of, 117
  final stage of, 40, 116–20
  final summary of, 112–15
  goal setting, 50, 118
  ground rules, 35–7
  initial assessment, 46–9
  length of, 33–4
  outcome evaluation, 107–12
  pace of, 34
  predictors of success/failure, 48
  problems with, 33
  sessions, 37–44
    blocking, 34
    case illustration, 130–44
    frequency, 35, 119–20
    punctuality for, 36
    style of, 41–2
    written accounts of, 42–4,
      112–15
Community resources, 120
Comorbidity, 12–13
Constructive activity, 92–3
Continuum, 71–5
Core beliefs, 17, 31–2, 52–3, 56–
    69, 70
  accessing, 61–9
  affective responses, 61
  changing, 32, 39–40, 70–80
  explaining to clients, 39, 59–60,
    145–6
  identifying, 61
  see also Schema
Criterion continuum, 73–4

DAPP-BQ (Dimensional
    Assessment of Personality

Pathology–Basic
    Questionnaire), 2
DAS (Dysfunctional Attitude
    Scale), 68–9
Data log, 77–8, 110
Daydreams, 64
DBT (Dialectical Behaviour
    Therapy), 13, 103–4
Dependent personality disorder, 8,
    12
  prevalence, 11
Depression, 3–4, 22–3
  cognitive behaviour therapy, 22
  cognitive biases, 24
  dysfunctional schema, 25
  negative automatic thoughts, 31
Diagnostic and Statistical Manual
    (DSM), 9–10
Diagnostic criteria, 1, 3, 5–9
Dialectical Behaviour Therapy
    (DBT), 13, 103–4
Diary keeping, 84, 85, 86, 109, 110
Dimensional Assessment of
    Personality Pathology–
    Basic Questionnaire
    (DAPP-BQ), 2
Drinking diary, 85, 86
DSM-IV (Diagnostic and
    Statistical Manual), 9–10
Dysfunctional Attitude Scale
    (DAS), 68–9

Early maladaptive schema, 19
Emotional disorders:
  cognitive theory, 24–5
  cognitive therapy, 22–5
Emotional instability, 53, 95, 102–
    5
Emotional suppression, 53–4, 103
    Employment, 83, 92–3
Environmental factors, 55

Feedback, 41–2, 112
Films, use in accessing core beliefs,
    68

Formulation, 26–7, 39, 46, 50–8,
      147–8
Frequency counts, 84
Friends of clients:
   feedback from, 112
   interviewing, 37, 47
   involving in treatment, 78–80

Goal setting, 50, 118
Ground rules, 35–7

Handouts, 39, 145–6
Historical test of schema, 75–7,
      149
History taking, 49, 52
Histrionic personality disorder,
      6–7, 12
   prevalence, 11
   sex differences, 11

ICD-10 (International
      Classification of Diseases), 9
Illiteracy, 55, 83, 92
Imagery, 63–4
International Classification of
      Diseases (ICD), 9
International Personality Disorder
      Examination Revised
      (PDE-R), 2
Interpersonal relationships, 27–8,
      78–80, 83, 90–1, 112, 120,
      see also Client–therapist
      relationship
Interviews:
   aims of, 47–8
   of clients, 46–7
   clinical, 2–3
   of friends/relatives of clients, 37,
      47

Labelling, 13-14
Life-threatening behaviour, 37, 54,
      95, 96–100
Literacy problems, 55, 83, 92

MCMI-III (Millon Clinical
      Multiaxial Inventory), 2
Meanings of events, 62–3
Measurement of change, 107–12
Media, use in accessing core
      beliefs, 68
Meditation, 103
Memories, 64
Millon Clinical Multiaxial
      Inventory (MCMI-III), 2
Mindfulness techniques, 103–4
Mood disturbances, see Emotional
      headings
Motivation, 48–9

Narcissistic personality disorder, 7
   prevalence, 10–11
Negative automatic thoughts, 24,
      31
NEO-PI-R, 4
Notebooks, 77–8, 110

Obsessive–compulsive personality
      disorder, 8
   prevalence, 11
Outcome evaluation, 107–12

Paranoid personality disorder, 5
   prevalence, 10
Parasuicidal behaviour, 37, 54, 95,
      96–100
Passive aggressive personality
      disorder, 12
   prevalence, 11
Patient assessment, 46–9
Patient feedback, 41–2
Patient–therapist relationship,
      27–30, 36–7, 41, 49–50, 63,
      117–18
PDE-R (International Personality
      Disorder Examination
      Revised), 2
PDQ-R (Personality Diagnostic
      Questionnaire Revised), 2

Personal care, 100–1
Personality diagnostic
    questionnaire revised
    (PDQ-R), 2
Personality disorder:
  assessment, 2–4
  classification, 4–5, 9
  cognitive models, 15–21
  comorbidity, 12–13
  defined, 1–2
  diagnosis, 1, 3, 5–9
  labelling patients, 13–14
  prevalence, 9–12
  sex differences in prevalence, 10,
    11
  types of, 5–9
Personality traits, 1–2
  fluctuation of, 3
  self-assessment of, 3
Positive data log, 77–8, 110
Prevalence, 9–12
Programmed behaviour, 15–16
Psychiatric disorders, 12, 95
Psychodynamic therapy, 13

Questionnaires, 2–3, 68–9

'Relationship laboratory', 28–30
Relationships, 27–8, 78–80, 83,
    90–1, 112, 120, *see also*
    Client–therapist relationship
Relatives:
  feedback from, 112
  interviewing, 37, 47
  involving in treatment, 78–80

Schedule for Nonadaptive and
    Adaptive Personality
    (SNAP), 2, 4
Schema, 2, 17, 19, 24–5, 31
  avoidance, 20
  compensation, 21
  early maladaptive, 19
  evidence for and against, 75–7
  historical testing of, 75–7, 149

  maintenance, 20
  reinforcement, 19–21
  see also Core beliefs
Schema questionnaire, 19, 69
Schizoid personality disorder, 5–6
Schizotypal personality disorder, 6,
    12
prevalence, 10
SCID-II (Structured Clinical
    Interview for DSM), 2
Self-caring, 100–1
Self-harm, 54, 95, 101–2
  increase of towards end of
    therapy, 119
Self-monitoring, 84
Self-report questionnaires, 2–3,
    68–9
Sex differences in diagnosis of
    personality disorder, 10, 11
Sexual abuse, 105–6
SIDP-R (Structured Interview for
    DSM-III-R Personality), 2
SNAP (Schedule for Nonadaptive
    and Adaptive Personality),
    2, 4
Social skills training, 89–90
Structured Clinical Interview for
    DSM (SCID-II), 2
Structured Interview for DSM-III-
    R Personality (SIDP-R), 2
Suicidal behaviour, 37, 54, 95,
    96–100
Supervision, 45

Temperament, 16
Therapists:
  behavioural contracts with, 91–2
  characteristics of, 30–1
  clinical supervision, 45
  relationship with clients, 27–30,
    36–7, 41, 49–50, 63,
    117–18
Therapy, different types of, 13, *see
    also* Cognitive therapy
Therapy sessions, 37–44
  blocking, 34
  case illustration, 130–44

frequency, 35, 119–20
ground rules, 35–7
punctuality for, 36
style of, 41–2
written accounts of, 42–4, 112–15
Thought records, 65
Time sampling, 84
Two-dimensional continuum, 74–5

Uni-directional continuum, 71–4

Work, 83, 92–3
Written accounts of therapy, 42–4,
112–15
Written formulation, 39